CONNECTING EUROPE AND ASIA

Security, Economy and Mobility

Edited by
Sihong Kim and Michael Reiterer

HU:iNE

Co-funded by the
European Union

"The European Commission support for the production of this Publication does not constitute an endorsement of the contents which reflects the views only of the authors, and the Commission cannot be held responsible for any use which may be made of the information contained therein."

Connecting Europe and Asia: Security, Economy and Mobility

Edited by
Sihong Kim and Michael Reiterer

Forward 1

Over the past decades, the Republic of Korea and the EU have built a strong partnership on shared values. Already in 2010, Korea and the EU elevated their bilateral relationship to a Strategic Partnership. The objective was not only to boost bilateral cooperation but also to join forces in addressing emerging regional and global challenges.

In 2021, the EU presented a new Strategy for cooperation in the Indo-Pacific. The strategy outlines a broad-based and inclusive approach targeting seven priority areas, including sustainable and inclusive prosperity, green transition, ocean governance, digital governance and partnerships, connectivity, security and defense, as well as human security.

As a likeminded partner at the forefront of digital innovation, Korea is a key partner and pivot state for further developing EU-Asia connectivity. With the adoption of the GDPR adequacy decision at the end of 2021, data can now flow freely and safely between Korea and the EU. The EU-Korea Digital Partnership will further galvanise joint cooperation on next generation technologies and standards. The EU and Korea are also forming closer links to accelerate the green transition as set out in their respective Green Deals.

Fostering greater connectivity requires major investments and a joined up approach. Therefore, the EU has launched 'Global Gateway' - a strategy to boost smart, clean and secure links in the digital, energy and transport sectors and to strengthen the health, education and research systems across the world. Between 2021 and 2027, the EU institutions and EU Member States, acting as a Team Europe, will jointly mobilise up to EUR 300 billion of investments in these priority sectors. The EU and Korea could work together in enhancing connectivity particularly in ASEAN countries.

Research and innovation underpin today's twin - green & digital

- transition. In 2022, Korea has expressed its interest to join Horizon Europe, the EU's main funding programme for research and innovation, as an associate member. This will open up many new avenues for joint research and innovation projects.

The Hankuk University of Foreign Studies (HUFS) and its Jean Monnet Centre of Excellence, led by Prof Kim Sihong, have played an important role in fostering academic and scientific cooperation between Korea and the EU. I am very grateful to Prof. Kim Sihong for his longstanding and unwavering dedication to building bridges between the academic world and policy makers in Korean and the EU. This book is a great example of this important work.

Maria Castillo Fernandez
Ambassador of the EU to the Republic of Korea

Forward 2

It is with my great pleasure to introduce the new book on 'Connecting Europe and Asia: Security, Economy and Mobility' co-edited by Professor KIM Sihong and Ambassador Michael Reiterer.

Connectivity - this is what the world needs today. Connectivity allows the European Union and Asia to work together for common goals. Both partners share objectives, resources, and know-how. New and better connectivity will boost growth and accelerate recovery from the pandemic. It will give more leverage to Europe and Asia in navigating unchartered waters in external relations.

The EU has extended its connectivity strategy from Asia to the globe through 'The Global Gateway' in 2021. In parallel - The EU's Strategy for Cooperation in the Indo-Pacific is under implementation and changing geopolitical configurations. The strengthened partnership between the EU and the Republic of Korea will help addressing common challenges. The Indo-Pacific strategy by Korea announced at the ASEAN summitry in 2022 will serve as a valuable platform for reinforcing connectivity between Europe and Asia.

This book explores a whole array of areas through which Europe and Asia can find common solutions and further collaboration for enhancing connectivity. From security and supply chain resilience to mobility and R & D, it illustrates sustainable ways to overcome challenges. It also underlines the strategic nature of promoting cooperation on connectivity between Europe and the Republic of Korea through institutionalization and agenda shaping.

This volume presents us with deep insight into the future of connectivity between Europe and Asia including Korea. It will be a stimulating guide for policymakers in the EU and Korea to broaden their future perspectives. I extend my warm congratulations and respect to Hankuk University of Foreign Studies (HUFS) and its Jean Monnet

Centre of Excellence led by Prof. Kim Sihong on its timely publication.

Chang-beom Kim
Former Korean Ambassador to the European Union
Advisor, Center for Strategic & Cultural Studies

Table of Contents

Connecting Europe and Asia
Security, Trade and Mobility

Sihong Kim

Introduction

The relations between Europe and Asia have developed ever since "Towards a New Asia Strategy" (1994) was prepared. Under this umbrella document, EU made a framework of agreements with individual states in Asia and the inter-regional dimension Asia Europe Meeting (ASEM) was introduced to fill the vacuum of nexus between Asia and Europe. Throughout more than two decades of inter-regionalism, there have been many improvement, starting from increasing volume of trade and mobility.[1] Nevertheless, due to changes in the international environment and concerns about power relations among stakeholders, a new horizon between Europe and Asia is highly demanded.

Main objectives of the EU Centre at HUFS (2019-2022) have been facilitating connectivity among the regions in concern by way of in-depth research activities, 1.5 Track diplomacy and opening to the civil society. *Connecting Europe and Asia* was a response to turbulent global challenges in which an illiberal international order and trade wars are imminent. It is believed that to fill this gap and to overcome the missing link between the two regions, it is imperative to increase level of connectivity in the areas such as security, trade and mobility, etc.

In 2016, EU Global Strategy referred to this issue in the name of "A Connected Asia" which put the emphasis on a direct connection between European prosperity and Asia security.[2] In fact, peace and stability in Asia are a prerequisite for European prosperity. This rationale was further developed with "Connecting Europe and Asia: Building Block for an EU Strategy" (2018). In East Asia, resurgent China and its Belt and Road Initiative (BRI) are creating uneasiness to security actors in the region. One of the reaction is manifested with Indo-Pacific Strategy among US, Japan, India and Australia, which is often called Quad. Against these backdrops, what Europe can do in the region is a theoretical as well as practical issue to be dealt with. Since 2019 was a time for advent of new leadership, it is appropriate to examine how Europe as security provider can engage in Asia. If more efficient and coherent leadership would be made, the role of the EU in Asia will accelerate to materialize different strategies. Besides, European states such as UK, France, Germany, Italy and the Netherlands recently published their own Indo-Pacific Strategies and the EU also prepared its own strategy towards the region.[3] In Connecting Europe and Asia Strategy, the European way via sustainable, comprehensive and rules-based connectivity is emphasized and respective strands between Europe and Asia are presented.

In 2021, the EU launched the Global Gateway as a counterweight to the BRI. Mobilising up to €300 billion by 2027, the initiative builds on several important steps the Union has taken in years. While its 2018 strategy expresses its will to cooperate with other regions to promote comprehensive, sustainable, and rules-based connectivity, the 2021 iteration provides concrete measures with corresponding financial foothold. To implement it, three ways are presented: connectivity as partnership, connectivity as an opportunity and connectivity as European sovereignty.[4]

In this introductory chapter we are firstly going to explore the historical overview of Europe-Asia relations in the post-Cold War era. Then more recent strategies of the EU will be explored such as EU Global Strategy, Connectivity, Global Gateway and Strategic Compass, etc. Third section presents summaries of each contribution of the book.

Connecting Europe and Asia

Connecting Europe and Asia is the basic concept of the Centre at HUFS. To comprehend better and deeper, it is appropriate to have a wide angle, comprising global and regional dimensions. As mentioned, Europe and Asia did a lot for this inter-regionalism, creating ASEM Process. It is true that economic and trade volume increased as anticipated in the 1994 Asia Strategy. Still initial expectations have become a kind of routine and therefore weakened the dynamics and the spirit of genuine inter-regionalism.

EU Global Strategy reinvigorated the relevance of the relations putting stress upon connectivity, starting from with China, ASEM and ASEAN. The Strategy also reiterated a more politically-rounded approach towards Asian security in collaboration with Japan, Korea, India and others. It argues non-traditional security issues such as anti-trafficking, migration, energy and maritime as well.

More concrete version of connectivity between Asia and Europe was introduced in 2018, that is, Connecting Europe and Asia Strategy. Here the European way via sustainable, comprehensive and rules-based connectivity is emphasized and three strands between Europe and Asia are presented: priority transport corridors, digital links and energy cooperation; connectivity based on commonly agreed rules and standards enabling a better governance of flows of goods, people, capital and services; by contributing to address the sizable investment gaps with EU's financial resources and international partnerships.

This project has strived in three particular areas of connectivity: security, economy and trade, and mobility. For its activities, the Centre has gathered the expertise from both home and abroad with high level of competencies. Academic, professional and governmental agencies were invited to provide added value and simultaneously to create 1.5 Track diplomacy in which activities of the Centre would contribute to the policy making and even law making processes.

Various events led to joint international activities and structural links with Asian and European academic institutions. For security connectivity, European experts on East Asia were invited as coordinators of the programme. For mobility connectivity, Chinese and Japanese universities were invited to participate and HUFS EU Centre shared invaluable networking experience among EU centers in Asia Pacific region including Japan, Taiwan, Hong Kong, Singapore, Australia and New Zealand during 2011-2015 period. EUSA Asia Pacific has been another important point of reference in that every year there is an annual congress attended by more than 200 scholars both from Asia and Europe who gather and share ideas on the process of European integration. HUFS EU Centre participates every year in these valuable events. These transnational linkages made and guaranteed a robust foundation for the successful activities of the Centre.

Openness to civil society has been another criteria every Centre has to keep in mind. HUFS EU Centre has various experiences with professional CEO associations, NGO, press associations and Chamber of Commerce Korea, etc. Hence some of the events were open to these groups and visibility of the EU was highly enhanced.

The followings are the main programs of the Centre activities during 2019-2022, which are divided into three pillars with interdisciplinary, multidisciplinary and transdisciplinary settings.

Security Connectivity between Europe and Asia

2019 will mark a critical and transitional year for Europe. With new leadership upon European Parliament election, there could be some instability and uncertainty, but could also yield positive dynamics. Connecting Europe and Asia from security point of view will examine in detail these transformations and try to figure out ways ahead. In particular, Belt and Road Initiative and Indo-Pacific Strategy will be analyzed with comparative perspective. To this end, maritime security will furnish a focal locus for whether the EU might engage in Asian security matters, without appearing to take sides. That would highly contribute to the promotion of a rules-based order and cooperative security initiatives.

Economic and Trade Connectivity

"Trade for All Strategy" in 2015 marked a quantum shift of economic concerns in Europe. More responsible trade and investment were highlighted. However, with the advent of Trump Administration, things changed drastically, causing issues such as illiberal international order, protectionism and trade war among states. In this aspect, FTA with East Asian partners are to be analysed and eventually to see if CJK FTA might be attainable with long term perspective. Economic and Trade connectivity will explore the possibility of further liberalisation through trade deals between Europe and Asia.

Connecting Europe to Asia in Mobility

Prospective relations among nations are guaranteed only with the mobility of younger generation in respective countries. Europe has been a vanguard in this realm and the Erasmus generation contributed further to the process of European integration. In Asia, a new mobility scheme called Campus Asia among China, Japan and Korea was introduced in 2012.[5] Unfortunately, however, due to historical and territorial disputes, implementation stalled. This section will explore a kind of exit strategy for this troubled situation in comparison with European experience. In the end, main focus will be centered on inbound mobility from Europe to Asian countries to make balance with outbound from Asia to Europe.

Summaries of book chapters

Michael Reiterer analyses the evolving process of the EU's external relations from Connectivity to Global Gateway and from Asia to the Indo-Pacific to build an inclusive international order. He argues that we are living in turbulent times. While the pandemic brought fears, restrictions and sovereign nationalism, we are indulging in more connections between Europe and Asia. Meanwhile Europe appears to be active in advocating an extension of its Connectivity Strategy from Asia to the globe through the Global Gateway. In parallel, the decade-long tradition of issuing diverse Asia strategies or Asia-Pacific policy papers is extended to the Indo-Pacific. The perception of the world seems to become larger. And the theatre for action is enlarged not only through Indo-Pacific Strategy but also with the Global Gateway and Strategic Compass. He contends that the EU wants to make it clear that it intends to engage and when necessary to compete. A value driven foreign policy needs not be ineffective. Rather, if an all-in and round up Team Europe approach is taken, appropriate means are given to build an inclusive international order in exercising strategic responsibility on a global scale. In conclusion, he argues that the lesson to learn if not already learned: the US is no longer the reliable and trusted partner to count on and therefore the EU should exercise strategic responsibility, whether it likes or not.

Lee Moosung presents new agenda and new methodology for connecting security between the EU and South Korea. The bilateral relationship between the EU and Korea is unique because both are the only partners, that have signed three agreements regarding political, trade and security. These agreements have paved the way for the two parties to interact in a more comprehensive, yet concrete, way to develop their bilateral relationship. Adopting the concept of normative power, he presents that the bilateral relations between the EU and Korea turns out to be normative, largely because the issues they are committed to address in a cooperative manner go beyond the scope and boundaries of traditional hard security concepts. For him, the methods connecting both parties as like-minded partners are also different from traditional ones. They include civilizing and normative methodologies and rules-based approach in tackling new emerging global concerns. In fact, both the EU and South Korea see adhering to these approaches as opportune and appropriate in this post-Westphalian or post-Cold War world security order. And it is on the basis of their ontological security-seeking that their material interests then seem to be accepted as appropriate.

Axel Berkofsky analyses Europe in the Indo-Pacific by examining the quality, impact and the shortcomings of recently published EU and European policy papers and strategies, mostly spelling out substantive and sustainable European contributions to security and stability in the region. According to him, these strategies have been written and published against the background of assertive and increasingly aggressive Chinese policies. So far, European attempts and aspirations to engage China politically and get Beijing to respect and implement international law have not worked. While self-declared resident power France approaches security in the Indo-Pacific to protect those 1.6 million plus French citizens permanently living in the region, Germany has continued to have the luxury of focusing on its trade and investment ties in the region. Berkofsky argues that though Germany sent a frigate it remains as a symbolic gesture at the maximum. In the German strategy towards Indo-Pacific, Berlin omitted to mention Taiwan in its policy guidelines and it looks like a conscious decision not to offend Beijing and avoid of being accused of interfering in Chinese internal affairs.

In presenting EU-East Asia connectivity, Ramon Pacheco Pardo adopts a perspective from theory to practice. Physical, digital, and people-to-people are the three areas that diverse strategies emphasize, particularly the first two. Chinese Belt and Road Initiative (BRI) of 2013 was forerunner and, to an extent, most other initiatives are either a response to BRI or have evolved in recent years as a result of Beijing's strategy. The EU is no stranger to this rush to connect the different parts of Eurasia. Throughout the recent endeavors the EU has taken, the principles are clear, cooperation with partners is essential. The EU has not been a relevant player in the region, but it has the potential to become one, particularly if it becomes a geopolitical actor. According to Pacheco Pardo, this will only happen if the EU moves from theory to practice. And the Global Gateway has the potential to address former shortcomings by providing the EU with the necessary financial muscle to implement its connectivity strategy, including towards East Asia.

Tereza Novotná examines the ways in which the EU and South Korea can cope with the conflict between the US and China both as the result of a shorter-term COVID-19 crisis and previous underlying long-term trends. She suggests that the EU should intensify cooperation with the Republic of Korea as the key country in North East Asia which is in a similar situation under the Sino-US strategic competition. It is imperative that the EU and ROK should: firstly, strengthen their Strategic Partnership, especially in the areas of common interest such as health, digital connectivity and climate change; secondly, identify areas where the EU and ROK can pre-empt escalation of the Sino-American rivalry by coming up with joint proposals that would be acceptable both to the US and China; and, thirdly, create a network of like-minded partners in South/South East Asia and Indo-Pacific including New Zealand and possibly Canada to offset any tensions from competition among power countries.

The expansion and deepening of global value chains (GVCs) underpinned international growth in recent decades. Kang Yoo-Duk tries to figure out current tectonic changes in GVCs in which the US, Europe and others are concerned with facilitating and consolidating the reshoring production regarding strategic resources. The term 'decoupling' has frequently been mentioned in both sides of the Pacific. Such an attempt will trigger the restructuring of existing GVCs that had followed the rapid growth of international trade up to now. The EU has been reorganizing its external policy with the vision of Open Strategic Autonomy. Besides, new factors have arisen such as climate, environment and human rights beyond traditional elements of price and technology. Under such circumstance and backdrop, both Korea and the EU should cooperate to restore the resilience of the free and open trade order. And these are to be reflected when both parties try to rewrite their free trade agreement.

According to Nicola Casarini, trade and investment have traditionally been the driving forces behind Europe-Asia connectivity. In due course, China has become the cornerstone of Europe's trade relations with Asia. Beijing accounts today for 11% in extra-EU exports of goods and has become the EU's second most important trading partner. Moreover, two-way investments have also surged. The long-standing tradition by the European Parliament (EP) to take a more critical position of China than other EU institutions demonstrates how Europe continues to be split on its China policy, since Brussels continues to oscillate between closer cooperation with the US on Beijing-related challenges and the pull of the Chinese market. Recent initiatives by the European Parliament seem to be advocating a temporary halt to EU-China connectivity, sharing some similarities with the US which is intent on decoupling from Beijing. Casarini argues that it remains to be seen whether the stance of the EP will prevail in Europe – or whether Brussels will continue to engage Beijing and eventually ratify the Comprehensive Agreement on Investment (CAI).

Kim Bongchul analyses mobility and educational cooperation between Korea and the EU. As globalization has stimulated the interaction and integration around the world, international mobility is the most active phenomenon including a variety of types of flows such as students, workers, refugees, and others. After presenting the EU mobility and higher education system including Bologna Process, he examines the lineaments of Korea-EU educational cooperation from historical viewpoints. For the latter, he presents the programmes Hankuk University of Foreign Studies (HUFS) has conducted for Korea-EU cooperation in education and research activities. The chapter concludes that more systematic cooperation and programmes should be created through continuous dialogue and discussion on the issue. The top priority would be to establish a system corresponding to the credit certification and qualitative certification systems commonly used in Europe. Considering that European higher education system is dualized into the EU Erasmus programme and the Bologna Process, Korea needs to pursue a bilateral approach of cooperation with the EU, its Member States, and non-EU Countries.

In presenting cooperation in science, research and innovation between Europe and Asia, Tomaz Wierzbowski firstly presents Europe's current endeavours. With only 7% of the world's population, Europe accounts for 20% of global R&D investment, produces one third of all high-quality scientific publications, and hold a world leading position in industrial sectors. To facilitate these developments, the EU has adopted Framework Programmes (FP) since 1984 and FP9 or Horizon Europe (2021-2027) which focuses on improving the objectives in the previous Horizon 2020, by supporting a broad range of member states science and research projects. Korea's participation in the EU's FP to boost research and innovation is still rather symbolic but has been increasing within every edition of EU's FP. This will change significantly if or when Korea becomes an associate country with Horizon Europe. The association will allow Korean entities to directly benefit from European funding schemes without joining the consortia led by European partners. This will also mean that the Korean government will contribute to European funds according to Korea's rate of participation. Recently both the EU and Korea agreed to prioritize cooperation in five thematic areas of ICT, Health/BIO, Climate Change and Emerging Future Technology, Research Hub, and Human capital development. In the 7th Republic of Korea-EU Joint S&T Cooperation Committee Meeting in 2022 both parties reaffirmed the above targets to be implemented in due time.

New Paradigms

To update and upgrade, we may consider the following in consideration with recent developments of global arena amid COVID-19. The forthcoming theme of the HUFS EU Centre(2022-2025) would be *New Paradigm for EU-Korea Relations.* By this, on the one hand, we are going to further develop existing bilateral relations under the three major frameworks: Framework Agreement (FA), Free Trade Agreement (FTA) and Framework Participation Agreement on Crisis Management (FPA). On the other hand, we are going to figure out how the EU and Korea can work together for regional and global cooperation. Autocratic and authoritarian regimes are threatening democracy and its institutions. Post-Cold War stability is in danger. Multilateralism is questioned and like-mindedness and natural partnership between the EU and Korea are under serious attack.

European Security Strategy (2003) was prepared at a time when external security threats were relatively absent. Meanwhile EU Global Strategy (2016) witnessed that peace and stability are not a given and therefore should not be taken for granted. In this situation the vision of Strategic Autonomy (2020) developed by the EU focuses on securing rules-based multilateralism in global governance and autonomous diplomatic actions based on shared values. Under the new global system of multi-polarity, Korea and the EU should find possible solutions to restore peace and prosperity. To overcome all by-products of the Sino-US rivalry, it will be imperative that like-minded partners cooperate together to find alternative ways of international order. The EU Centre hopes to make a small but significant contribution to this cooperation by way of research and policy oriented activities.

The main theme of the Centre is the *New Paradigm for EU-Korea Relations.* By this, the Centre is going to review both the historical development and ongoing issues of cooperation from global, regional, and bilateral points of view. It is necessary for us to meet many new challenges in the fields of economy, ecology, human security, global governance and peace. In this context, we propose three areas of research activities of the Centre; 'From Connectivity to Global Gateway', 'Securing Resilience in Global Supply Chain between Europe and East Asia', and 'EU-Korea@60'.

The *New Paradigm for EU-Korea Relations* will be the basic concept of the Centre at HUFS. To provide a comprehensive answer to the concept, it is necessary to understand the new paradigm that has changed international society. The structural tension between United States and China has been growing and changing global landscapes in several issues. The recent crisis in Ukraine and unilateral invasion of Russia shows the looming threat of a New Cold War, while COVID-19 pandemic showed clearly that global cooperation is only way to overcome global challenges. In this context, we are witnessing that the venue for cooperation between the existing global actors and other middle powers became more comprehensive, and accordingly, opportunities for regional and global cooperation expanded even more. In this situation where the paradigm shift of the new international relations is underway, the relationship between the EU and Korea needs to be upgraded and revised, along bilateral, regional and global dimensions.

This book project has been a product of the Jean Monnet activities.

Throughout the development, we have witnessed that connecting Europe and Asia has a long way to go, given that strategic rivalry and change of the global supply chain, due partly by COVID-19, are now delving into new horizon. Therefore, we, sharing common values of democracy, rule of law and human rights, should engage and further facilitate free and open international order-making.

What remains to be done are common efforts to materialise such orders into concrete circumstances. HUFS Jean Monnet Centre of Excellence will no spare efforts to meet these goals, with our new agenda in the coming years being *New Paradigm for Korea-EU relations.* By this, we intend to build blocks for peaceful and prosperous world based upon rules-based international order. We expect that Korea and the EU, being likeminded, can do better. They are optimal partners to each other in fulfilling their respective interests and therefore in contributing to a better, safer, and more prosperous world.

---

1 Kim Sihong, "EU's External Relations with South East Asia". International Area Review, 2007, Vol. 10, No. 2, pp. 40-41.

2 Kim Sihong, "EU Global Strategy and Korea-EU Relations", Journal of Contemporary European Studies, 2017, Vol. 35 No. 3, pp. 40-41.

3 Kim Sihong, "The EU's External Policy: Multipolarity, Strategic Autonomy and Indo-Pacific Strategy", Journal of EU Studies, 2021, No. 59, 2021, pp. 233-234.

4 Miguel Berger, "Why connectivity can strengthen European sovereignty", December 2, 2021.

5 Kim Sihong, "Regional and Inter-regional Education Processes in East Asia and Europe", Journal of South-East Asian Studies, 2012, Vol. 22 No.1, pp. 6-7.

Connecting Europe and Asia

From Connectivity to Global Gateway, from Asia to the Indo-Pacific – building an Inclusive Liberal International Order

Michael Reiterer

Introduction

We are living in interesting times: While the pandemic brought restrictions, isolation and boosted nationalism, we are talking about more connections between Asia and Europe in terms of security, trade and mobility? Are we out of step or doing the right thing in acting anti-cyclical?

Europe appears to be particularly active in advocating an extension of its Connectivity Strategy (JOIN 2018) from Asia to the globe through The Global Gateway (JOIN 2021, 30 final). In parallel, the decade-long tradition of issuing various kind of Asia strategies or Asia-Pacific policy papers is extended to the Indo-Pacific (JOIN 2021, 24 final). The perception of the world seems to become larger, not narrower.

Thus, the theatre for action is extended not only through the Indo-Pacific Strategy but also through the 'Global Gateway'. Concerning the latter, Africa (Murphy 2021) profited the most as the Indo-Pacific Strategy includes "only" East Africa. The 2022 EU-Africa Summit confirmed the goal "to boost public and private investment building on existing initiatives and partnerships." (Sixth 2022) The President of the European Commission, Ursula von der Leyen, put a price tag of "at least EUR 150 billion for Africa for the next seven years. This is the first package under our Global Gateway Strategy." (von der Leyen 2022) Concerns about the contents and structure of Chinese agreements with African countries, the "debt trap" and/or lack of transparency and sustainability raised concerns (Areddy *et al.* 2021) and prompted action.

Becoming a global player?

While this seems to be in line with the EU's strong position in global trade, investment, official development aid, humanitarian assistance, rules and standard setting (Brussels effect) and thereby influencing global governance, it raises the question whether the EU is able and willing to devote the means necessary to actually become a more effective global player. Global players have to demonstrate the capacity to actively cover many tasks in content and geographical scope at the same time; for the EU the times of "economics only" are gone.

Moving from soft to smart power, adding a more traditional security dimension implies not only a learning process for the EU but is also a development requiring the change of a mind-set. The EU has embarked on this trajectory in discussing various concepts such as 'strategic autonomy'. A more recent addition to the debate is the Strategic Compass (Council Nov. 2021) defining common European threat scenarios (Borrell 2021). While the Compass takes up the ball from the 2016 Global Strategy the construction processes this time has been quite different: member states were deeply engaged with the European External Action Service (EEAS), while the Global Strategy was also the brainchild of external actors like think tanks.

During the five years since 2016 the world has changed considerably, not only because of COVID-19. What has not changed, however, is bad luck for the EU when announcing major policies: The Global Strategy suffered from the all-dominating news about BREXIT, the announcement of the Indo-Pacific Strategy was overshadowed by AUKUS, the Australian – UK - US security arrangement in the Indo-

Pacific leaving the EU and France in particular in the cold. The UK appears to be the link between these two events!

Taking up global challenges

As for the changes we note the continued raising of China's assertiveness beyond the Belt and Road Initiative (BRI): Hongkong and Taiwan are synonyms to which a growing nuclear arsenal and the modernisation of the People's Liberation Army in particular its navy in view of the claims in the South China Sea and the fortification of artificial islands have to be added. Thus, the **systemic challenge** becomes more pronounced. These aspects also determine the US position and intensify the strategic Sino-American competition. Avoiding choosing sides or hedging has become part of diplomacy worldwide but is especially pronounced in the Indo-Pacific. As a consequence, alliances are weakened as they are no longer all-encompassing but become sectoral. The 'Asian Paradox', good economic but strained political relations at the same time, comes to its limits.

With the two initiatives quoted, Indo-Pacific and Global Gateway, the EU is opting for taking up these global challenges and not to withdraw to Europe or to its near-abroad only. As a result, the EU will have to spend more political and economic capital to cover both, its home-turf and the globe.

This is necessary as the US clearly indicated that its Pivot.2 to the Indo-Pacific following Pivot.1 of the Obama Administration has as a consequence a withdrawal from other areas where allies are expected to step in. The catastrophic exodus from Afghanistan was a very visible sign of US retreat from an area. The US will also pay less attention to the extended European neighbourhood. In order to avoid a vacuum, the EU will have to step in and up. The US will be confronted with anxieties amongst its allies and partners in the Middle East, who will doubt whether they can still rely on Washington's support and protection. The EU too will be anxious as to whether it can and should take over tasks of burden sharing, especially at times of crises.

Consequently, more engagement will be necessary and more means will have to be made available to meet the challenges in the near and far abroad. The test came unexpectedly and massively: On 24 February 2022 Russia invaded the Ukraine. The EU moved quickly with sanctions, the financing and delivery of weapons and upgraded their military expenses massively. Seen positively, this could become an opening for the EU in world politics where it can play according to its strengths and experience.

This is also in the interest of Europe: As lesson learnt from the pandemic, supply and value chains need a strategic analysis. This should not result in "de-globalisation" but to adaptions that ideally lead to a better cooperation and more security. Such functional cooperation would be particularly important in the health sector – while still struggling with the COVID-19 pandemic and its ever-changing variants, we already have to get ready for the next one, now. Without going back to the devastating plague of the Middle Ages, just to recall the Spanish Flue, HIV, MERKS and Ebola – pandemics seem to come in shorter intervals and heightened effectiveness of mutations. The link with reducing the living space of animals, the loss of biodiversity, the link to climate change adds to complexity but also underlines the need for cooperation and to withstand the temptation of ineffective populism and nationalism advocating isolationism.

To take up the theme of the conference (Connecting Europe and Asia: Security, Trade and Mobility), organised to commemorate the 10th anniversary of the Jean Monnet Centre of Excellence at HUFS, **non-action** would reduce security, trade and mobility! This in turn would lead to loss of efficiency, further economic recession, increase poverty and widen the already dangerously big gap in societies, national and international. These cleavages within societies are endangering societal coherence world-wide: the 'January 6 attack' on the Capitol in the US, the weakening of the value consensus in Europe, the split among those opposing or promoting vaccination – with the all-out attack of Russia on the existing political and legal order on top. In Asia, geopolitics causes autocratic leaderships to progress, nationalism to strife, democracy to retreat ... all developments heightening the burden for like-minded partners to maintain a cooperative order.

The Global Gateway and the Indo-Pacific Strategies appear to be a sort of chicken and egg case. The common denominator certainly is the push for engagement. This fulfils a double function: first, to unite the EU, Member States and institutions behind these ideas of openness and to act together as "Team Europe" in EU-speak. Second, a message to partners, whether like-minded or not, that the EU is prepared to play a larger role and will continue to build networks in line with Europe's norms, standards and values.

The EU playing a larger role does not refer only to a military dimension. Military engagement and hard ware have always been an important yardstick in Asia, which has made the EU look less relevant on security issues. However, the EU stands for comprehensive security with 'European characteristics'. It is much wider in scope, covering effective multilateralism, rule of law and is human and values-based. Despite this different focus, which is important to acknowledge, this does not mean that security or the military dimension is blended out. On the contrary, all these elements are part of the concept of comprehensive security and are interlinked and have been strengthened because of the attack by Russia.

The development of the Strategic Compass should clarify this and therefore is an important undertaking. A highly complex operation with its own tensions and pit-falls, it attempts to create a pan-European threat evaluation and a European security culture which enables politicians to live up to the promises of engagement in providing security to the EU citizens, to strengthen the resilience of the EU, in cooperation with interested partners. It should also transmit the clear message that security bears a price tag too. President Putin was the highly successful salesperson for this endeavour in attacking the Ukraine, driving also Finland and Sweden in the arms of NATO.

From 'strategic autonomy' to 'strategic responsibility'

It is significant that at the same time NATO is undergoing its own review, NATO 2030, which should lead to a new Common Strategy at the Madrid Summit in June 2022. This should help to facilitate cooperation between the EU and NATO to achieve complementarity, not to indulge in competition. Therefore, the term **"strategic responsibility"** should be further used to get rid of the misunderstandings created by the talk about strategic autonomy, especially in the context of NATO. This would also signal the EU's willingness for burden sharing.

Uniting strengths and capabilities are also necessary to prevail in the systemic competition with autocracies as a joined-up approach by the like-minded increases effectiveness. Therefore, an Indo-Pacific leg should be added to the long-standing Transatlantic dimension of cooperation with the US in which interested and like-minded partners should join in the spirit of openness.

I was glad to note that eight months after our recommendation in the CSDS Policy Brief (Pacheco Pardo *et al.* 2021), "Deputy Secretary of State Wendy R. Sherman and European External Action Service Secretary General Stefano Sannino led the first U.S.-EU high-level consultations on the Indo-Pacific on December 3, 2021 in Washington. The two reviewed their respective Indo-Pacific engagement and strategies. Both reaffirmed their intention to work together and with partners in support of a free and open Indo-Pacific that is inclusive, based on the rule of law and democratic values, and contributes to the stability, security, and sustainable development of the region. The United States and the European Union share a strategic interest in strengthening cooperation with partners in the Indo-Pacific on the basis of shared values and interests, and in support of multilateral rules-based frameworks. Both sides reaffirmed the importance of ASEAN centrality and supporting a strong and independent ASEAN." (EEAS 2021)

Enhancing security needs the cooperation of as many of the willing as possible. There can be no exclusiveness or binary option if we are to establish a just international order that is reliable, sustainable and resilient. Therefore, ASEAN centrality is important, as would be the admission of the EU to the East Asian Summit to strengthen this centrality through multilateralism. At the same time, this confirmation and the above-quoted Joint Press Release put at least from the EU perspective into doubt the adequacy of the mini- or plurilateral approach of the Quad or AUKUS in the larger Indo-Pacific context, both without the EU and ASEAN, the banner bearer of multilateralism.

From the Liberal to the Inclusive Liberal International Order

We used to refer in this context to the **'Liberal International Order'** (Reiterer 2020) built on values and institutions. However, the term "liberal"[1] leaves states that fear being left behind or those like China that have not participated in its creation, suspicious. In the latter case, this is ironic given that China tends to forget that this order was instrumental for its rise. Nevertheless, China is a revisionist power and aims at a state dominant order with the Chinese Communist Party as the driving force within the state. To mitigate this concern, a new narrative for an '**Inclusive** Liberal International Order' is needed, where connectivity and a larger geographical ambit, as reflected in the transition from Asia to the Indo-Pacific and from Connectivity to Global Gateway covering additional partners, plays a key role. Such an inclusive order would be built on the foundation and achievements of the Liberal one, its values and institutions. However, the focus would have to shift to the themes of the future and – as reflected in the growth of minilateral (Atnassova-Cornelis *et al.* 2021) and plurilateral institutions – become more inclusive and representative in its membership. The G7 seeks a new licence of life in extending invitations to global partners, like Korea. This enlarged membership would in turn link back to the goals to pursue, the means to use and accentuate the need for institutional reform, with the United Nations as an outstanding example. Again, the Russian attack on the

Ukraine underlines the need for UNSC reform, especially when one of the five permanent members is party to a conflict.

Through such an approach 'strategic responsibility' would get an additional dimension and should not be limited to the EU but include its eleven strategic partners. Without taking responsibility it will not be possible to find solutions, responsibility to be shared by all as many problems of the future are often the consequence of the unsolved problems of the past. The COVID-19 pandemic has added itself and also serves as a magnifier, catalyst or booster.

However, in order to avoid giving the wrong impression that the Inclusive International Order would abandon the values on which it is built and given the massive attack on the order by Russia through its illegal war of aggression against the Ukraine after having already illegally annexed the Crimean Peninsula in 2014, both "inclusive" and "liberal" should be used.

The joint declaration by China and Russia, "on the International Relations Entering a New Era and the Global Sustainable Development" prepared for the meeting Xi-Putin at the occasion of the opening of the 2022 Beijing Winter Olympic Games, clearly advocates "transformation of the global governance architecture and world order; there is increasing interrelation and interdependence between the States; a trend has emerged towards redistribution of power in the world; and the international community is showing a growing demand for the leadership aiming at peaceful and gradual development." (Joint Statement 2022) The Russian war of aggression and the reticence of China to condemn it, mocks their Joint Statement which refers 16 times to 'peace' and disqualifies their advocacy of a new order:

> "The sides call on all States to pursue well-being for all and, with these ends, to build dialogue and mutual trust, strengthen mutual understanding, champion such universal human values as peace, development, equality, justice, democracy and freedom, respect the rights of peoples to independently determine the development paths of their countries and the sovereignty and the security and development interests of States, to protect

the United Nations-driven international architecture and the international law-based world order, seek genuine multipolarity with the United Nations and its Security Council playing a central and coordinating role, promote more democratic international relations, and ensure peace, stability and sustainable development across the world."

A network of digital partnerships

In line with network diplomacy connectivity partnerships, digital partnership could be geographically enlarged and linked up with other groupings like the G7 and G20. This would be important in terms of efficiency too: if there are too many parallel initiatives, ideas will not be translated into actions. Projects dead at birth undermine the credibility of its originators.

Some concrete examples to illustrate this dilemma:

The G7 came up, under US leadership, with the Build Back Better World Initiative (B3W) "to help meet the tremendous infrastructure need .... to collectively catalyse hundreds of billions of dollars of infrastructure investment for low- and middle-income countries in the coming years." (The White House 2021). At the same time the G7 participants France, Germany, Italy, and the EU should also commit financially to the EU Global Gateway.

A like-minded partner like Japan, is running its own 'Partnership for Quality Infrastructure' (Berkofsky 2019), initially providing US$110 billion for financing the construction of roads, railways and ports as part of its Free and Open Indo Pacific Program; this project was also reflected in the G20 Principles for Quality Infrastructure Investment (MOFA Japan 2019). Bilaterally, the EU and Japan concluded in 2019 a Partnership on Sustainable Connectivity and Quality Infrastructure. The Japan–United States Strategic Energy Partnership (JUSEP) (Paskal 2021) aims at turning Japan into a strategically important energy hub providing related infrastructure in the region.

Korea as guest of the G7 is part of the B3W pledge, but has also

> promised to deliver under its own New Southern Policy Plus scheme which enlarged at the 2020 Korea-ASEAN summit its previous engagement in adding seven more areas of cooperation (Kim 2021, Pacheco 2021).

Can it be realistically expected that in times where measures to overcome the effects of COVID-19 and huge commitments for financing the climate transition require enormous amounts of capital, that there will double or triple financing of programs by the mentioned participants? Unfortunately, we will have to add a Marshall-Plan-type funding to rebuilt the Ukraine after the war has ended.

Although the Chinese BRI has turned out not to be as glorious as it has been heralded and perceived initially, it is still effective in countries which are not interested in values-induced conditionality, despite often lacking sustainability and profitability. Furthermore, BRI helps not only to export Chinese products and services but norms and standards. This is part of China's more assertive policy exercising economic statecraft; in fact, standards have become policy instruments of competition. China is no longer content being a 'norm taker' but also wants to be a 'norm maker', no longer exercising normative power through the power of example – China has not been very successful in projecting soft power - but seizing "'discourse power' (话语权) and offering 'China solutions'" (Mattlin 2021) as part of its contestation of the Liberal International Order. Therefore, real engagement in terms of financial commitments is necessary, for credibility and effectiveness.

Acting decisively and effectively would add a positive dimension to the narrative of an "Inclusive Liberal International Order". Therefore, there is need for a networked diplomacy which turns the various schemes, programs and initiatives into building blocks for an **Inclusive** International Order.

From Connectivity to Global Gateway
A wake-up call for Asia

Key elements covered by the Global Gateway are elements already familiar from the Connectivity Strategy: digital transition, clean energy transition, transport, people-to-people connections, and trade and resilient supply chains.

Before turning to the Global Gateway, we should recall, that the 2018 Connectivity Strategy was specifically designed as Euro-Asian connectivity, after a thorough mapping process with results published in 2017. In parallel, the Asia Europe Meeting (ASEM) had provided a comprehensive definition of connectivity (Annex 1 2018) and launched in 2018 the ASEM sustainable connectivity portal that helps to measure progress in terms of connectivity and sustainability based on 49 indicators. The 13th ASEM Summit in Cambodia recommended timely information sharing on projects and the mainstreaming of connectivity into all relevant ASEM activities (Council, The Way Forward 2021) in order to achieve results.

Asia has to be on the look-out: The EU-ASEAN joint ministerial statement on connectivity of December 2020 pledged cooperation in "recognising the unique experience of connectivity and regional integration of ASEAN and the EU" (Council 2020). In the East-Asian context one has to add the above-mentioned partnership with Japan as well as the EU-China connectivity platform. However, this overall priority advantage of the Connectivity Strategy for Asia could get lost through Global Gateway, if no implementing actions are taken for the Connectivity Strategy.

An EU-Korea Connectivity Partnership
Complementary cooperation

Connectivity partnerships with Japan and India have suffered so far from a lack of implementation – this not because of a lack of ideas but most likely systemic in the sense of a clash of administrative cultures. The modus operandi of administrations within the EU is often creating problems when implementing projects, whether in regional policy or in research: public tenders are handled differently, administrative practices have a strong cultural touch. These differences are multiplied in interregional cooperation. While a mapping of these differences could be a long-term project, complementarity horizontally or vertically could be the solution. Horizontally in working side-by-side in a coordinated manner on an integrated project while every partner pursues its own project. (Example: while one partner builds a hospital, the other one the training centre for nurses). Vertically, connecting parts of a problem: While one party builds the port infrastructure, the other one links the harbour with the mine by road, train or boat. As an additional benefit, the mobilisation of the private sector will be easier in concentrating on a well-circumscribed project with one project manager. This could be called 'complementary cooperation'.

In practical terms, the EU and Korea should undertake a mapping of know-how, experience, means available and interests to be pursued, prior to deciding the topic and the geographic area where they cooperate in complementarity to achieve best synergies.

The following are some pointers to possible projects the strategic partners EU and South Korea could take up in form of a cooperative connectivity partnership:

- The pilot project on **cyber security** got under way and could be accelerated with concrete actions points, for instance concerning an EU-driven defence and sanction mechanism against identified cyber aggressors.
- Korea is interested to further develop Incheon as an Asian **aviation**

hub; post-pandemic the quick implementation of the bilateral aviation agreement and its link with the first regional aviation agreement the EU has agreed with ASEAN.

- After consolidation of the bilateral EU-Korea partnership its enlargement to a **trilateral one with ASEAN** would add a regional dimension and, important, strengthen ASEAN and its claim to centrality. At the same time this would serve as a stepping stone to Global Gateway.
- The management, redesign and adaption of **production and value chains** is no longer an add-on to trade policy but could become the centre of a connectivity partnership based on a risk analysis and a mapping process identifying the areas where closer cooperation would be mutually beneficial, which obviously will include the health sector; within trade the special focus on the delivery and export of services is an area of mutual interest and eventually benefit.
- In the **people-to-people dimension** the cooperation in academic education could be intensified in making the academic systems more compatible (recognition of degrees). In the spirit of Erasmus + cooperation with the EU inspired Campus Asia could be enhanced based on best-practice exchanges.
- A special focus should be put on **emerging technologies and high-tech**, which would lead organically to enhancing cooperation in **R&D** where Horizon Europe offers ample possibilities to finance joint endeavours. Korea should finally become an associated member of the program. **Vocational training** and relevant exchanges are another means of technological cooperation which so far has not got much attention. In drawing on its high degree of connectivity and high-speed internet services, South Korea took the lead in online teaching – an area which will survive the pandemic. Education in the large sense could become part of Hallyu and profit from the highly experiences cultural managers.
- A connectivity partnership would be an excellent preparation for Global Gateway which will enlarge the connectivity program

beyond Asia with **Africa** as the main profiteer. Given the successful development of Korea it has a high level of positive recognition and could team up with the EU which has in turn experience on the African continent and will launch a special cooperation project with Africa.

Global Gateway

All these elements could feed into the Inclusive Liberal International Order whose participants should be as comprehensive as possible. However, given the mentioned attacks on the Order and the alternative models promoted by China and Russia, it should not turn 'value-free'. In this respect "Global Gateway" is refreshingly clear in its opening sentence, "Democracies – and the values that underpin them - must demonstrate their ability to deliver on today's global challenges." (JOIN 2021) In contributing to meet these global challenges, the EU wants to move closer to being seen as a global actor, through investment in digital, transport, energy and trade projects.

Thereby the Global Gateway enlarges the traditional EU approach of focussing on standard setting in formulating six key principles which have to be met when financing development projects: i) democratic values and high standards; ii) good governance and transparency; iii) equal partnerships; iv) green and clean; v) security-focused; vi) catalysing private sector investment.

Working with like-minded partners will be a key element, as the goal is "to create links and not dependencies" as President von der Leyen put in the 2021 State of the Union Address (von der Leyen 2021).

Although these principles need further refinement, they point into a direction where the EU has more credibility, experience and effectiveness, namely global governance building, including the 'Brussels effect' for norm and standard setting. This approach looks more promising, because upon reflection, one could also ask whether eight years after China started its BRI drive and the EU's de-facto reply in 2018 with its Connectivity Strategy for Asia, whether following the infrastructure direction shown by China is the most effective policy line for the EU to take. Although the EU's method is broader and values based, is the financing of global infrastructure projects the area where the EU can be most effective and successful, where it enjoys the highest credibility?

A concrete example: From a value-perspective, stemming the backlash against democracy should be a common task, in the interest of the people to enjoy their rights and as part of the systemic competition with authoritarian regimes. However, working exclusively with democracies (Summit for Democracy by President Biden) to achieve democracy is the wrong approach: democracy and multilateralism are the goals. The largest possible number of those willing should be invited to join the journey towards democracy in the sense of 'leaving nobody behind'. As poverty kills democracy, development projects need to be designed to implement the UNSDGs to overcome poverty, leading to the above mentioned Inclusive Liberal International Order. Global Gateway projects realising the above mentioned six principles should fall into this supportive category.

One has to recognise that since the presentation of the Connectivity Strategy in 2018 when the then HRVP Mogherini claimed that this Strategy was no reaction to any other initiative, the Global Gateway was announced quite differently by EC President von der Leyen in her 2021 State of the Union address: "We will build Global Gateway partnerships with countries around the world. We want investments in quality infrastructure, connecting goods, people and services around the world. We will take a values-based approach, offering transparency and good governance to our partners. We want to create links and not dependencies!" (von der Leyen 2021) The addressee became clear: "We are good at financing roads. But it does not make sense for Europe to build a perfect road between a Chinese-owned copper mine and a Chinese-owned harbour. We have to get smarter when it comes to these kinds of investments" - a clear swipe at the Chinese BRI (European Views 2021).

While this sounds as if BRI were put in the category of 'systemic rival' in the sense of the tryptic of the 2019 EU-China Outlook (European Commission 2019), it is potentially a hybrid case, where cooperation on concrete projects should be possible in the common interest.

In pursuing its policies based on the Connectivity Strategy and the Global Gateway as well as on its Indo-Pacific Strategy, the EU should not fall into the trap of seeing everything through the Chinese prism: (Reiterer 2021)

- Offering interested partners a platform and a network of wide-ranging cooperation possibilities is an important contribution to enlarge the room of manoeuvre for others and opening a path to more autonomy for them.
- The EU in turn would profit from this cooperation in gaining strength and continue to influence global governance. The strategic partner, Korea, shares many of these interests with the EU and the already broad cooperation between the two should be deepened in implementing the Connectivity and Indo-Pacific Strategies as important stepping stones for the Global Gateway.

How to feed the animal?

Last but not least, implementation hinges on financing. The EU can draw on the 2021-27 Multiannual Financial Framework and link it up with other projects like the Trans-European Networks, the planned digital networks and some resources could be found from the Green Deal – an indication of rebranding existing frameworks. However, more than 40 billion euros to be spent on technology and infrastructure (Nardelli 2021) will not be easy to mobilise.

Although the **IP-Strategy** refers to various European financial institutions, like the European Investment Bank and the European Bank for Reconstruction for financing. They can with the support of the European Fund for Sustainable Development incentivise the private sector to contribute and mobilise more funds. This is necessary as both initiatives, Connectivity and Global Gateway are doomed, if they do not provide/attract adequate financing. This would weaken the EU's position to the point of making it irrelevant in this crucial policy sector and wreck efforts to become a recognised international player.

Global Gateway aims at creating investments of up to €300 billion between 2021 and 2027 in a joint approach by Member States, European financial institutions, national development finance institutions and most importantly, the private sector not only in terms of resources but also expertise. Measured against the $1,2 – 1,3 trillion China is estimated to spend on its BRI until 2027 (Chatzky *et al.* 2020) and the G20 estimate of a global infrastructure investment deficit of €13 trillion by 2040, which translates into €1.3 trillion every year if climate and environmental requirements are added, the €300 billion – one fourth - look less impressive. The all-important soft power element explained above would be an important complementary element for the EU's enlarging role and the Inclusive Liberal International Order.

Conclusions

In trying to find answers to the introductory questions, this chapter has shown the consequences of the successive expansion of the policy fields from Asia to the Indo-Pacific and to the global level. Thereby the EU wants to make it clear that it intends to engage and when necessary to compete. A value driven foreign policy needs not be ineffective if an all-in Team Europe approach is taken, adequate means are appropriated to build an Inclusive International Order in exercising strategic responsibility on a global scale within the limits posed by finite resources. Unity shown in the face of Russian aggression augurs well in this respect, although it will be difficult to maintain over an extended period of time.

While the connectivity train has already left the station, the EU in consultations with its partner should continuously reflect, in which domains and geographical areas they can best pursue their interests while playing to their strengths – following others is not necessarily the best option. Connectivity partnerships should become part of networks at the various regional levels to eventually reach a global scale. Differences in administrative cultures have been neglected and should be factored in when designing collaboration in a manner that each partner works independently but both are complementing each other through this 'complementary cooperation' approach. The ability of handling differing administrative procedures is often the decisive element whether an operation turns out to be a success or failure. The other decisive element, financing power, might become even more decisive, if President Biden is not able to deliver on his infrastructure and climate change promises because of resistance within the Democratic Party. Lesson to learn if not already learned: the US is no longer the reliable and trusted partner to count on blindly – the EU has to exercise strategic responsibility. If there were any doubts, Putin effectively destroyed them.

A personal remark to conclude: I have experienced over the last decade that the HUFS Jean Monnet Centre of Excellence has contributed greatly not only to raising awareness in Korea but also in stimulating intellectual discussion on how to find a common pathway for the EU and Korea. Therefore, I wish to record gratitude, appreciation and best wishes for the future to the team and its leader Professor Kim Si-hong who has been instrumental for this success.

---

1 The Liberal International Order is also under duress in Europe (Hungary, Poland); a thorough discussion is beyond the scope of this chapter. See Higgott 2022 for a masterly discussion of the development and challenges of liberalism and the values it stands for.

Bibliography

"Annex 1 to ASEM Summit in Ulaanbaatar 2018, ASEM Connectivity," *ASEM Info Board.* https://cdn.aseminfoboard.org/documents/Annex_I.pdf

Areddy, James, and Bariyo, Nicolas. "Uganda Finds China's Leverage Is in the Fine Print of Its Lending." *The Wall Street Journal*, December 27, 2021. https://www.wsj.com/articles/uganda-finds-chinas-leverage-is-in-the-fine-print-of-its-lending-11640601003

Atanassova-Cornelis, Elena, and Pejsova, Eva. "Minilateralism: an opportunity for the EU's engagement in the Indo-Pacific," *CSDS Policy Brief* Nr. 22/2021. https://brussels-school.be/publications/policy-briefs/policy-brief-minilateralism-opportunity-eu%E2%80%99s-engagement-indo-pacific

Berkofsky Axel. "Tokyo's 'Free and Open Indo-Pacific': quality infrastructure and defence to the fore," *Real Instituto Elcano*, ARI 34/2019, March 14, 2019. http://www.realinstitutoelcano.org/wps/portal/rielcano_en/contenido?WCM_GLOBAL_CONTEXT=/elcano/elcano_es/zonas_es/asia-pacifico/ari34-2019-berkofsky-tokyos-free-and-open-indo-pacific-quality-infrastructure-defence-fore

Borrell Josep. "A Strategic Compass for Europe," *Project Syndicate*, November 12, 2021. https://www.project-syndicate.org/commentary/eu-strategic-compass-by-josep-borrell-2021-11

Chatzky Andrew, and McBride James. "China's Massive Belt and Road Initiative," *CFR Backgrounder* 100, January 28, 2020. https://www.cfr.org/backgrounder/chinas-massive-belt-and-road-initiative

Council of the European Union. "The Way Forward on ASEM Connectivity," ASEM 13 Summit in Cambodia, November, 25-26, 2021 via videoconference. https://www.consilium.europa.eu/media/53138/the-way-forward-on-asem-connectivity.pdf

Council of the European Union. "A Strategic Compass for Security and Defence - For a European Union that protects its citizens, values and interests and contributes to international peace and security," 13638/21, November 9, 2021. https://i2.res.24o.it/pdf2010/Editrice/ILSOLE24ORE/ILSOLE24ORE/Online/_Oggetti_Embedded/Documenti/2021/11/11/st13638_en21%20SC%20DRAFT%200.pdf

Council of the European Union. "EU-ASEAN joint ministerial statement on connectivity," December 1, 2020. https://www.consilium.europa.eu/en/press/press-releases/2020/12/01/eu-asean-joint-ministerial-statement-on-connectivity/

European Commission. "EU-China – A strategic outlook," March 12, 2019. https://ec.europa.eu/info/sites/default/files/communication-eu-china-a-strategic-outlook.pdf

European External Action Service (EEAS). "EU-U.S.: Joint Press Release by the EEAS and Department of State on the High-Level Consultations on the Indo-Pacific," December 3, 2021. https://eeas.europa.eu/headquarters/headquarters-homepage/108366/eu-us-joint-press-release-eeas-and-department-state-high-level-consultations-indo-pacific_en

European Views. "With its 'Global Gateway', the EU is upping the pressure on China's BRI," October 13, 2021. https://www.european-views.com/2021/10/with-its-global-gateway-the-eu-is-upping-the-pressure-on-chinas-bri/

Higgott, Richard. "Confronting Global Challenges to Liberal Values: It is not too late yet, but...," *CSDS, In Depth*, 01/2022. https://brussels-school.be/publications/other-publications/confronting-global-challenges-liberal-values-it-not-too-late-yet

Joint Communication to the European Parliament, the Council, the European Economic and Social Committee, the Committee of the Regions and the European Investment Bank. "The Global Gateway," JOIN (2021) 30 final, December 1, 2021. https://ec.europa.eu/info/sites/default/files/joint_communication_global_gateway.pdf

Joint Communication to the European Parliament and the Council. "The EU strategy for cooperation in the Indo-Pacific", JOIN (2021) 24 final, September 16, 2021. https://www.eeas.europa.eu/sites/default/files/jointcommunication_2021_24_1_en.pdf

Joint Communication to the European Parliament, the Council, the European Economic and Social Committee, the Committee of the Regions and the European Investment Bank (2018). "Connecting Europe and Asia - Building blocks for an EU Strategy," JOIN (2018) 31 final, September 19, 2018. https://eeas.europa.eu/sites/default/files/joint_communication_-_connecting_europe_and_asia_-_building_blocks_for_an_eu_strategy_2018-09-19.pdf

"Joint Statement of the Russian Federation and the People's Republic of China on the International Relations Entering a New Era and the Global Sustainable Development," February 4, 2022. http://en.kremlin.ru/supplement/5770

Kim, Sea Young (Sarah). "How the 'Plus' Factor in South Korea's New Southern Policy Plus Can Ensure Sustainability," *KEI The Peninsula*, September 9, 2021. https://keia.org/the-peninsula/how-the-plus-factor-in-south-koreas-new-southern-policy-plus-can-ensure-sustainability/

Mattlin, Mikael. "Normative economic statecraft: China's quest to shape the world in its image," in *The Routledge Handbook of Chinese Studies*, ed. Chris Shei, and Weixiao Wei. Routledge, 2021. https://doi.org/10.4324/9780429059704

Ministry for Foreign Affairs, Japan. "G20 Principles for Quality Infrastructure Investment," Osaka Summit on June 28 and 29, 2019. https://www.mof.go.jp/english/policy/international_policy/convention/g20/annex6_1.pdf

Murphy, Theodore. "The EU's Global Gateway and a new foundation for partnerships in Africa." *ECFR Commentary*, September 29, 2021. https://ecfr.eu/article/the-eus-global-gateway-and-a-new-foundation-for-partnerships-in-africa/

Nardelli, Alberto. "EU to Lay Out $46 Billion Technology Plan to Counter China". *Bloomberg*, November 11, 2021. https://www.bloomberg.com/news/articles/2021-11-11/eu-to-lay-out-46-billion-infrastructure-plan-to-counter-china

Pacheco Pardo, Ramon. "With new middle power comes great responsibility for South Korea". *CSDS Policy Brief* no. 24/2021. https://brussels-school.be/sites/default/files/CSDS%20Policy%20brief_2124_0.pdf

Pacheco Pardo, Ramon, and Reiterer, Michael. "The EU and the US in search of Common Ground: Extending the Transatlantic to an Indo-Pacific Partnership?" *CSDS Policy Brief* no.4/2021. https://www.korea-chair.eu/wp-content/uploads/2021/04/CSDS-Policy-brief_2104.pdf

Paskal, Cleo. "Indo-Pacific strategies, perceptions and partnerships: The view from seven countries." *Chatham House, Research Paper*, March 23, 2021. https://www.chathamhouse.org/2021/03/indo-pacific-strategies-perceptions-and-partnerships/07-japan-and-indo-pacific

Reiterer, Michael. "A China policy is not an Asia policy, but no Asia policy is without a China policy". *Policy Briefs*, 2021/50, Global Governance Programme, EU-Asia Project, Europe in the World; EUI. https://cadmus.eui.eu/handle/1814/72925

Reiterer, Michael. "The EU Defending Global Governance, the Liberal International Order, Providing Security: The Relevance for the Asia Pacific," *Asia-Pacific Journal of EU Studies*, Vol. 18 No. 1, 2020; pp. 1-19.

"Sixth European Union - African Union Summit: A Joint Vision for 2030," 18 February 2022. https://www.consilium.europa.eu/media/54412/final_declaration-en.pdf

The Nation. "Uganda may lose only international airport over Chinese loan," November 27, 2021. https://thenationonlineng.net/uganda-may-lose-only-international-airport-over-chinese-loan/

The White House. "Fact Sheet: President Biden and G7 Leaders Launch Build Back Better World (B3W) Partnership." June, 12, 2021. https://www.whitehouse.gov/briefing-room/statements-releases/2021/06/12/fact-sheet-president-biden-and-g7-leaders-launch-build-back-better-world-b3w-partnership/

von der Leyen, Ursula. "Opening speech by President von der Leyen at the 6th European Union-African Union Summit" 17 February 2022. https://ec.europa.eu/commission/presscorner/detail/%20nl/speech_22_1142

von der Leyen, Ursula. "State of the Union 2021," European Commission, September 15, 2021. https://ec.europa.eu/commission/presscorner/detail/en/speech_21_4701

Connecting security between the EU and South Korea[1]

New Agenda and Methodology

Moosung Lee

Introduction

The bilateral relationship between the European Union (EU) and South Korea is both unique and remarkable. It is unique because the EU and South Korea are the only partners, which have signed the Framework Agreement, the Free Trade Agreement, and the Strategic partnership Agreement. These agreements have indeed paved the way for the EU and South Korea to interact in a more comprehensive, but yet concrete, way to develop their bilateral relationship.

The relationship is also remarkable in terms of the way both partners (re)identify the issues of mutual concern and the methods in coping with new challenges in this new Cold War era. The common agenda of problematic security issues the EU and Korea are committed to tackle needs an unconventional approach. While military security is arguably the main concern for the EU and also for South Korea even in this era, this does not necessarily exclude non-traditional security concerns, such as economic wellbeing, the protection of human rights, environmental protection, and fight against terrorism. They are now new, but key, subjects for securitization, if and when they affect our very own existence.[2] That is why we cannot disregard the reality in which competition and conflicts between (state) actors are inevitable, which is the innate feature of international relations.[3] At the same time, we still face a new reality created by the end of the Cold War: a new security environment came to the fore, forcing us to pay renewed attention to the issues that used to be side-lined. Global economic relationship is arguably one of its kinds. The salience of global economic relationship appears remarkable, particularly when the acceleration of globalization, and the intensification of economic competition, cause economic insecurity across borders. Environmental protection and the protection of human have become important and they are the core values that the EU, among others, seeks to protect. Reflecting this new security environment and the concerns of international society, the cooperation between the EU and South Korea deserves discussion, not least to establish how best to enhance their connectivity.

These issues of common interest are more inclusive in nature than before, and they are addressed in a normative nature. The EU and South Korea see the peaceful resolution of conflicts through regional cooperation and integration as appropriate and even instrumental.[4] Unlike the realist approach that puts too much focus on the strength of military capability in addressing security issues, the EU, as well as South Korea in pursuing their strategic partnership agreed that experimenting with regional cooperation in addressing regional security issues is worthwhile. Therefore, both parties agreed to sign a so-called strategic partnership, hoping this, if applied to traditional inter-state relationship marked by conflicts according to realist perspective, to help regulate the otherwise conflictive inter-state relationship. This is indeed a new, if not innovative, way, if compared with the traditional form of, e.g., an alliance. While the latter assumes there is an enemy to fight against, the former does not assume the dynamic of inter-state relations in a similar way, but rather understands and approaches international conflicts in a more neutral way.

Keeping all this in mind, this chapter aims to study the connectivity between the EU and South Korea in both hard and soft security, asking in what ways, and to what extent, this would actually affect the EU's normative stance in world politics, as well as South Korea's commitment to help the EU realize such a political objective. The chapter also argues that given the specific features associated with the issues and methods the EU and South Korea have adopted, we can also possibly contend that a wider window of opportunity for cooperation will not only be opened, but in the process the EU is able to reflexively represent itself as a novel kind of actor.

The chapter is composed of four sections. In Section Two, we will discuss the EU's normative feature, as well as its implications for its relationship with Korea. Based on this theoretical argument, Section Three delves into the methods both parties agree to adopt in dealing with issues of mutual and global concerns. Section Four examines the ways the EU and South Korea address a variety of security issues either through their joint participation in the KEDO program or through crisis management operations. Section Five provides the summaries of the argument by discussing the implications of this study.

EU as a normative power

The EU is a novel kind of actor that promotes a new world order. The world older that it seeks to promote is different from the one that we previously used to know. It is not the Westphalian order. When the Westphalian world order prevails, it is the physical survival of states that is a top priority; but the very action to realize such a material objective intensifies inter-state conflicts. After the horrible experience of two times of war on the European continent, some of the countries in the region began to think that it is the establishment of the post-Westphalian order that could help come to terms with the Westphalian order, and bring about peace and prosperity to Europe.[5] Yet this does not necessary mean that the EU turns a blind eye to the hard security issue itself. Instead of solely focusing on the hard security issue, it seeks to extend its security concerns, ranging from human rights, environmental protection to the health governance, to name but a few. By bringing these soft-security issues onto the global agenda, the EU seeks to highlight new security concerns of post-Cold War era; by doing so, it attempts to go beyond the current dynamic of international relations marked by power politics.

With these political and historical objectives and imperativeness in mind, regional cooperation aiming at conflict resolution has been experimented with, first, among Western European countries, and then among Central and Eastern Europe countries which have been brought into the EU's fold through successive enlargements.[6] In the process, the EU has been created, and it has since then evolved to function as a new political entity that is not solely based on military power nor economic wealth. Instead, the EU seeks to identify itself as a 'power over opinion', focusing on an ideational nature of politics and governance characterized by common principles, while disregarding power politics, a feature of the Westphalian world order.[7] The implication is that irrespective of whether it has power or wealth, the value of the EU lies in the extent to which it has an ability to shape what passes for normal in world politics. This, as Diez argues, is also what differentiates the EU from other forms of normative power such as the US: the former is reluctant to rely on military power in diffusing its norms and values, whether it has it at its disposal; but the latter is ready to do so, if it feels it necessary.[8] For this objective, the EU has developed a hybrid polity in which both supranational and intergovernmental forms of governance co-exist and also a particular political-legal constitution in which it is able to determine its international normative identity.[9] The attack by Russia on the Ukraine has, however, given a strong impetus for the EU to accelerate its move towards a common defense policy.

Of course, discussing the concept of normative power Europe entails the examination of its ontological self. Yet what is as much important at this juncture is what constitutes its 'being'. If so, the subsequent question is how its so-called 'normativeness' is reflexively represented. It is for this objective that we are now going to discuss the way in which its normative self-identification is represented in both its external relationship in general and its relationship with South Korea in particular. For this objective, we will address this issue, focusing on the role to be played in its external relationship.

According to Holsti, it is necessary to examine national roles played by states in order to make sense of their individual foreign policy choices, if we assume it as a critical variable in the operation of the international systems.[10] Yet, unlike the initial position that the foreign policy roles of states is a function of policy-makers' beliefs and domestic politics, Wendt expanded this argument. Thereby he made a constructivist contribution, and focused on role identity of states, arguing that it would determine one's relationship with significant others.[11] That is, if the identity is a property of intentional actors that generates motivation and behavior dispositions, the relationship among actors would be dependent on the intersubjective understanding of parties involved in interaction.

The EU represents itself as a normative power as of now, and its external relations could thus be understood in a similar manner. Unlike the realist approach of international relations which asserts protecting one's physical and material interests as a paramount priority, thereby making inter-state conflicts inevitable in international relations, the EU's concerns and focus lies elsewhere. Given its horrible experiences of wars, it seeks to overcome such an embedded erstwhile statist ontological position. Its focus has been how to overcome the Hobbesian culture that prioritizes the survival of states and renders conflicts among them inevitable. To overcome such a gloomy prospect innated in the statist ontology, the EU has been created, and experimented to create a new culture (Kantian culture) so that parties concerned could share common value and ideas, and therefore form their corresponding interests.[12]

As a way to realize such a solemn political objective, the EU has emphasized the ways to refurbish our perception of what matters as key values and methods to practice them in our daily lives – whether they are political, economic, and social ones. So, the EU has sought to address a wide range of issues, whether they are directly related to national security, or whether they are deemed as indirectly related security issues (such as human rights promotion, environment protection, and the like, as the result of the broadening and deepening of the security agenda). With these grand political, ethical, and moral objectives in mind, the EU has experimented with new foreign policy instruments, such as strategic partnership, as well as the new idea of conflict resolution through regional cooperation and integration. Therefore, we shall discuss their specific features and implications in turn.

The EU's normative methodologies

The EU has forged its foreign relationships, emphasizing the normative appropriateness. To demonstrate the normative features, the EU has accommodated such policy instruments as regional cooperation and strategic partnership. While the regional cooperation method has long underpinned both the EU's domestic politics and foreign relations, the strategic partnership has recently been tried as a new policy instrument when the common foreign and security policy has been adopted as its second pillar. Of these, unsurprisingly, the strategic partnership is not unique for the Union. It is also used by other countries, such as China, but examining its inherent feature would arguably indicate that partnership diplomacy along with policy for regional cooperation are appropriate forms for foreign policy, befitting with the EU's normative traits.

The promotion of its experience of regional cooperation aimed to conflict resolution is the first subject for discussion.[13] By emphasizing the regional cooperation-and-regional conflict-resolution nexus, the EU has attempted to consolidate its normative identity both internally and externally. As far as its internal politics is concerned, the EU holds the firm belief that instead of relying on such a traditional form of coalition, like a military alliance, cooperation at the level of low politics is both appropriate and instrumental for further cooperation in area where such sensitive issues as military and national security would otherwise be hard to address. This so-called spill-over effect has indeed made a positive contribution to the peaceful coexistence among the otherwise conflictive European states, if the history of Europe is any guide.[14] More interestingly, the plan to extend European integration beyond Europe appears to arrive at "more generic portfolio of propositions about the dynamics of integration in any context".[15]

To be sure, there are caveats especially if the normative approach based on regional cooperation is to be understood solely from the functionalist perspective. In order for this approach to be operational, there are two preconditions to be met. On the one hand, those participating in the regional framework should ensure their compatibility of political, economic and social systems. This, as Deutsch argued, is a prerequisite for a successful security community.[16] That is perhaps why western European countries did not even try to integrate with, e.g., the Soviet Union during the Cold War era, given their incompatibility of political, economic, and social systems. It is also with such preconditions in mind that the EU seeks to ensure that its members accommodate and develop the so-called Copenhagen criteria. They reflect the core normative basis by which the Union is able to identify itself as a normative power and then to differentiate itself from others.[17]

The EU has also sought to export its regional cooperation and conflict resolution methods to the other parts of the world. One of the cases in point is its promotion of regional cooperation in Asia, as was clearly spelled out in its Asia policy communications, such as 'Towards a new Asia Strategy'.[18] By doing so, the EU can influence regional integration elsewhere both actively and passively. On the one hand, it is able to compel actors to change their behavior by providing incentives through financial support, preferential market access, or the provision of technical expertise, or by putting pressure on actors, such as making regionalization a condition for development assistance. On the other hand, it can also passively influence others which attempt regional cooperation simply by its existence. When the EU becomes a model for other regional actors, it is also able to influence others' behavior, and it is able to affect others, but in passive way.[19]

Yet it is still necessary to note that the interaction and engagement of parties concerned would not necessarily lead to the change in the nature of culture in which they interact. To be sure, there was once a hope that the Hobbesian culture that makes conflictive inter-state relations inevitable would also be transformed either into a Lockean culture when cooperation among actors would be eventually conducive to the realization of their material interests, which in turn binds them together, or even into a Kantian culture where participants see each other as like-minded partners which accommodate and promote common interests and values. While all this seems to be a plausible scenario, however, there were also unintended consequences dampening such a hope. That is, the more states meet, ironically, the more likely they realize that they are not only different, but also dangerous to each other. If so, they then eventually come to perceive each other as an abject other which poses an ontological security threat. Thus, when the differences they found do not remain as they are, but are presented as a source of ontological security threat, they, then, would immediately be entrapped by an ontological security dilemma. Under these circumstances, to safeguard their self-identity, they would act in such a way as to distinguish themselves and others and make them willing to compete or even conflict with the others that aim to preserve their own ontological security.[20]

The strategic partnership adopted by the EU could also be seen as an instrument representing its normative identity. By creating a social space where it engages in role-playing to assert its international normative identities, the EU is able to enhance its status and prestige in international society. Thus, Vahl argues that it would in fact make us aware of both the importance and relevance of normative discourse in this world.[21] More specifically, if all this helps us understand the value and ideas, which makes the world different from the one that we, for example, used to know during the Cold-War era, new opportunities are opened, which not only seem to be urgent, but at the same time commonsensical. It is to this that the EU makes its own contribution, as the framework of strategic partnership provides a social space that appear to make all this possible. Therefore, the EU's strategic partnership functions to provide an arena in which actors engage in role-playing to assert their international identities and enhance their status and prestige as global actors. We tend to expect socialization within the strategic partnership framework in which actors are able to "gain recognition for their status and position in the international system through competitive role-play with a significant Other".[22] If so, it is imperative to take seriously the normative implications the EU-Korea strategic partnership would have with particular reference to their cooperation in areas of high politics, such as military security, and how it would then affect the EU's efforts to consolidate its normative identity in the process.

Although the strategic partnership has been regarded as the main foreign policy instrument, it could also be understood differently, depending on how the geopolitical challenges the EU has to face are related to key elements in its diplomatic practices.[23] So, Smith outlines three different images of partnership diplomacy, namely, strategic, managerial, and reactive. First, when a strategic image of partnership diplomacy is concerned, it is possible to argue that there is a guiding framework in line with an EU grand strategy. Second, as regards the managerial image, it concerns a view that emphasizes the ways in which the EU has developed a differentiated and adaptive version of partnership diplomacy. Last but not least, when it comes to the reactive view, one also has to consider a view that highlights the position of the EU in which there is a reaction to events rather than a principled or pragmatic approach.[24]

Despite all these debates, however, it is important to argue how the EU and Korea see each other as like-minded partners, and what kind of roles they would expect from each other when they are called on to play their own roles, particularly, through the methods promoted by the Union. If so, the strategic partnership can become a glaring example to discuss the extent, and the way, the EU can be projected as a 'force for good' and also as a normative contributor to world order.[25]

Connectivity through Security Cooperation

1. KEDO

The cooperation between the EU and Korea in the area of military security dates back to the time when the North Korean nuclear issue came to be posited as a source of grave international concern. Prior to the bilateral cooperation in security areas, the EU's concern towards the Korean peninsula became concrete when North Korea asked for external help to overcome the consequences of the flood that hit North Korea hard back in 1994. Since then, the EU has also engaged in this international emergency aids programs. When the EU first interacted with North Korea, it immediately realized that security issues could not be properly addressed without dealing with the embedded structural problems that had already aggravated North Korea's economic situations. Therefore, the EU got directly involved in the North Korean security issues through political dialogues, while also maintaining its constructive engagement in a broader context.

The first official occasion through which the EU and South Korea met was their joint participation in the Korean Peninsula Energy Development Organization (KEDO) program. The KEDO was once understood as the very regional framework where conflict transformation was attempted. Created to address hard security issue, it directly dealt with the North Korean nuclear issue. Based on the key objective of the KEDO programme, the first institutionalised form of regional cooperation (before strategic partnership was agreed upon), it became operational in 1995 primarily based on the initial trilateral partnership among the US, South Korea and Japan. While the program was initially launched by involving these three key stakeholders, discussions to expand their membership soon started. At first, there were disagreements. While South Korea wanted to keep KEDO membership limited, the US and Japan had a different idea for different reasons. The US needed further sponsorship in addition to the three founding countries, considering that they were not able to provide full financing for the KEDO projects. Japan, however, wanted to develop the KEDO with a broad international membership for its domestic political reasons.[26]

Despite the initial disagreements among key stakeholders, the EU was invited in 1997. Given its prior experience and knowledge about the issue of non-proliferation under its Euratom program, the EU's participation appears appropriate.[27] To be sure, whether the EU proved committed to addressing the North Korea issue still invites controversies: this was largely because the core member countries of the EU disagreed with the KEDO's approach. This brought the cohesiveness issue to the fore in discussing its external relationship. More specifically, Germany was reluctant to approve the KEDO's Light Water Reactor program promised to be provided under the KEDO program, as its domestic politics was then dominated by the anti-nuclear, and therefore anti-LWR, platform, largely led by the Greens. Compared to the case of Germany, there were both similarities and differences as far as the French position was concerned. France had a strong aversion to any interaction with North Korea, especially pointing to its human rights practices that were not in line with its traditional position towards human rights.[28]

Despite all the difficulties, however, all the existing participants at least on appearance agreed to start the framework agreed upon in 1994 with a promise of the construction of a light water reactor targeted for completion in 2003. The EU also expressed its commitment when invited as an executive member. It promised to provide 500,000 metric tons of heavy fuel oil annually, until the entrenched animosity between the US and North Korea destroyed the very process itself in 2006. Yet it was the EU's participation that in a sense raised awareness of the North Korean issue in a region where it was not a priority.[29] If that is the case, we can also argue that the regional framework provided by the KEDO program demonstrated the EU's normative feature, if its normative identity is not so much determined by rational choice, but by the logic of appropriateness: the logic of appropriateness here denotes the commitment on the part of the EU to address the issue of hard security based on dialogues and engagement, not necessarily through armed forces.

Apart from their shared KEDO programs, both parties also seem to act as like-minded partners in other forms of framework. For example, when the Six-Party talks were created and replaced the KEDO in the wake of the 2003 nuclear crisis, the cooperation between the EU and Korea was an issue of interest. For many reasons, the EU was not invited, and remains outside this framework, but it has nonetheless continuously expressed its interests in Korean affairs. For all the vicissitudes of the Six-Party Talks in terms of its continuity and effectiveness, the Talks are now stalled. Even so, it is still important to note the position of the EU that has at least indirectly supported the key role of this framework, and whenever it is possible, the necessity of resuming such talks.[30]

2. Crisis Management Operation

The EU and South Korea are geographically remote and do not see each other as a critical stakeholder. Yet they are still a potential, and also important, partner for cooperation in the future, given their commitment to democracy, a market economy, human rights and the rule of law. While they share certain values and ideas befitting to the features of this post-Cold War era, they also cooperate in addressing global security issues through the framework of crisis management operation. It is within this framework that both parties are now able to address both hard and soft security issues in a more systematic manner.

The glaring example for this objective is the joint military exercise to fight against maritime piracy. It was the military cooperation in the Atalanta Operation or European Union Naval Force (EU NAVFOR) Somalia that demonstrated how both were well connected in cooperation for hard security. As both parties jointly engaged in a counter-piracy operation to protect vessels and monitor fishing activities off the coast of Somalia for naval security, they also made a significant contribution to the protection of ships and people off the coast of Somalia.[31] This was indeed a military operation subsumed under the crisis management operation. The Crisis Management Participation Agreement (CMPS), which signed in 2014 and entered into force 2016, functioned as a security pillar in a broader context of strategic partnership. To the extent that the main objective of the CMPS is to allow both parties to cooperate in the fields of peace-keeping operations or humanitarian operations, both the EU and Korea are able to take substantial actions tackling some security issues, some of the focus area of crisis management. This is rather different from the roles expected within the existing frameworks of political cooperation, which focuses on institutionalized dialogues. It is through this agreement that they see each other as new partners who are able to cooperate to address new security challenges that seem to be critical in this post-Cold War era.

It is also interesting to note here that the missions in which the EU and South Korea are jointly involved in are different from the previous forms of military exercise. They combine military and civilian features. This combination of the methods used in dealing with a variety of issues which makes their approach and cooperation different.[32]

As a matter of fact, the CMPS has been operated autonomously from NATO. As we would normally know that NATO is the primary framework for military cooperation as far as the hard security issue is concerned, the framework provided by the CMPS is one where the EU and South Korea would rather bring to the table a number of other kinds of global security issues, such as promoting effective multilateralism.[33] That is why even when the heads of states and governments met in Helsinki in December 1999, and decided to improve the EU's crisis management capabilities with the establishment of an army corps of 50,000-60,000 troops, its military mission was not solely aimed at military operations.[34] On the contrary, there was questions of whether their crisis management operations include military forces or not, they still sought to guard the civilian feature of CMO for two reasons. First, because peacekeeping operations or humanitarian intervention subsumed under the CMPS entail some normative features in terms of the methods and objectives that they use and look after. It is also because its military mission has almost always been linked with its civilian mission, such as policing, institutions building, security sector reform, and the like: although their military mission is often criticised as ineffective, its mission is still valuable, because the way such operations have been undertaken is in fact chimed in with its normative identity.

This difference, furthermore, also makes their connectivity unique and remarkable. In this manner the EU can present itself as a different kind of actor through its partnership with like-minded countries, such as South Korea.

Conclusion

We have examined the connectivity between the EU and South Korea with particular reference to their cooperation in areas of hard security. While the theme, hard security, itself, may connote their potential entrapment in the realist perspective, the examination of their actual pathway of realizing such a foreign policy objective rather proves to be normative in nature. The reasons for their relationship to be normative are twofold.

First, the bilateral relationship turns out to be normative, largely because the issues the EU and South Korea are committed to address in a cooperative manner go beyond the scope and boundaries of traditional security concepts, if we assume the context we are focusing on is not necessarily an anarchical international system where conflicts between actors (most largely states) are inevitable. It is on the one hand due to their mutual recognition that political cooperation is necessary in order to address a wide range of new political issues in this post-Cold War era: they both appear to agree that new security agenda has been deepened and widened, and it is not only hard security issues, but other soft security issues also have to be securitized. Therefore, such issues as human rights, free markets and multilateralism, science and technology, education, climate change, and development assistance have become new referent objects to be secured.[35] It is in this way the EU has responded and acted in addressing global concerns.

This is also on the other hand how the EU acts in such a way as to serve the interests of international society, not necessarily for their narrow self-interests with the support of its partner, South Korea.[36] Therefore, we should not define the EU as the traditional form of actors we see in today's international system where power politics among state actors prevail, but the relationship it seeks to forge and develop should be different. That is why the focus of their cooperation could be characterised as inclusive, rather than exclusive, in the sense that not only hard-security issues, but soft ones have become the subjects for cooperation.

Second, the methods connecting both parties as like-minder partners are also different. Unlike the traditional ways of dealing with hard-security issues, more civilizing, and rather normative, ways and methodologies have been employed. In addition to their common concerns of an inclusive nature, both the EU and Korea also agreed to adopt the rule-based approach in tackling new global concerns. The rule-based approach primarily stresses the importance and appropriateness of dialogues and engagement. This is also the reflexive representation of the EU's deontological ethics, if it is an integral part of its normative (or more correctly ethical) feature.[37] Given that a deontological approach that emphasizes the rationalization of duties and rules, which guides the EU in its external actions, the Union should then reason and rationalize its external actions through processes of engagement and dialogue.[38]

Hence, this is in a sense the way the EU may promote its constitutive principles as actions and policies in world politics. That is also one of the underlying reasons why an institutionalized rule-based approach has underpinned their demarche to make the world (in general) and the Korean peninsula (in particular) safer and prosperous. While critical views remain and die hard, questioning their very effectiveness, both the EU and South Korea still see sticking to them as opportune and appropriate in this post-Westphalian or post-Cold War world security order. To be sure, all this would not necessarily mean that their choices are the mere reflection of the fact that both actors are not military strong. Instead, it is a normative reflection of the fact that this is how they are able to safeguard who they are.

1 This chapter is a revised and upgraded version of Lee, Moosung, "Connecting security between the EU and South Korea: New Agenda and New Methodology", The Journal of Contemporary European Studies, 2022 40:1 1-12.

2 Barry Buzan, Ole Weaver and Jaap de Wilde, *Security: A new framework for analysis* (Boulder: Lynne Rienner Publishers, 1998), 21-48.

3 For more, see neorealists' argument, such as Kenneth Waltz, *Theory of International Politics* (London: Addison-Wesley Publishing Company, 1979).

4 Moosung Lee, "The EU, regional cooperation, and the North Korean nuclear crisis," *Asia Europe Journal* 14, no. 4 (2016): 401-415; Thomas Diez and Nathalie Tocci, The EU, *Promoting Regional Integration, and Conflict Resolution*, ed. (Basingstoke: Palgrave Macmillan, 2017).

5 Falk, Richard, "A 'New Medievalism'?," in *Contending Images of World Politics*, eds. Greg Fry and Jacinta O'Hagan (London and New York: Routledge, 2000): 106-116.

6 Atsuko Higashino, "For the Sake of 'Peace and Security'? The Role of Security in the European Union Enlargement Eastwards," *Cooperation and Conflict* 39, no. 4, (2004): 347–368.

7 Ian Manners, "Normative power Europe: a contradiction in terms?," *Journal of Common Market Studies* 40, no. 2 (2002): 239.

8 Thomas Diez, "Constructing the Self and Changing Others. Reconsidering `Normative Power Europe'," *Millennium: Journal of International Studies* 33, no. 3 (2005): 620-623.

9 Manners, "Normative power Europe: a contradiction in terms?," 240-242.

10 K. J. Holsti, K. J., "National Role Conceptions in the Study of Foreign Policy", *International Studies Quarterly* 14, no. 3 (1970): 234.

11 Alexander Wendt, *Social Theory of International Politics* (Cambridge: Cambridge University Press, 1997): 224-247.

12 Wendt, *Social Theory of International Politics*, 246-312

13 Diez and Tocci, *Promoting Regional Integration, and Conflict Resolution*.

14 David Mitrany, "The prospect of integration: Federal or functional," *Journal of Common Market Studies* 4, no. 2 (1965): 119–149.

15 Ben Rosamond, "The uniting of Europe and the foundation of EU studies: revisiting the neofunctionalism of Ernst B. Haas," *European Journal of Public Policy* 12, no. 2 (2005): 243.

16 Karl W. Deutsch, *Political Community and the North Atlantic Area. International Organization in the Light of Historical Experience* (Princeton, NJ: Princeton University Press, 1957).

17 Diez, "Constructing the Self and Changing Others. Reconsidering `Normative Power Europe'," 629.

18 European Commission, "Toward a New Asia Strategy. COM (94) 314 final," European Commission, documented July 13 1994 in Brussels, https://eur-lex.europa.eu/legal-content/EN/TXT/PDF/?uri=CELEX:51994DC0314&from=EN. (accessed 3 December 2012).

19 Moosung Lee and Thomas Diez, "Introduction: the EU, East Asian conflicts, and the norm of integration," *Asia Europe Journal* 14, no. 4 (2016): 358.

20 Jennifer Mitzen, "Anchoring Europe's civilizing identity: habits, capabilities and ontological security," *Journal of European Public Policy* 13, no. 2 (2006): 270-285.

21 Marisu Vahl, "Just good friends? The EU-Russian 'Strategic Partnership' and the Northern Dimension." *CEPS Working Document*, no. 166 (March 2001): 1-55.

22 Anna Michalski and Pan, Zhongqi Pan (2017), "Role Dynamics in a Structural Relationship: The EU-China Strategic Partnership," *Journal of Common Market Studies* 55, no. 3 (2017): 612.

23 Micheal Smith, "The geopolitics of the EU's partnership diplomacy: strategic, managerial or reactive?," *International Politics* 56, no. 3 (2019): 288-303.

24 Smith, "The geopolitics of the EU's partnership diplomacy: strategic, managerial or reactive?," 290.

25 Michael Smith and Huaxian Xie (2010) "The European Union and China" The Logics of 'Strategic Partnership'," *Journal of Contemporary European Research* 6, no. 4 (2010): 435.

26 Charles Kartman, Robert Carlin and Joel Wit, "Policy in Context: A History of KEDO 1994-2006," June 2012 (Standford: CISAC, 2012), 53.

27 Moosung Lee, "The EU, regional cooperation, and the North Korean nuclear crisis," *Asia Europe Journal* 14, no. 4 (2016): 405.

28 Kartman, Carlin and Wit, "Policy in Context: A History of KEDO 1994-2006," 54.

29 Naoko Aoki, "KEDO: How multilateral cooperation helped an unprecedented North Korean project," *CISSM Working Paper*, September (2017): 6.

30 Lee, "The EU, regional cooperation, and the North Korean nuclear crisis," 404-406.

31 Ramon P. Pardo, Linde Desmaele, and Maximilian Ernst, "EU-ROK relations putting the strategic partnership to work." KF-VUB KOREA Chair Report (October 2018), p. 5. https://www.ies.be/files/EU-ROK_RELATIONS.pdf. (accessed 5 December 2021).

32 Hae-won Jun, "EU-ROK in Crisis Management Operations," Nicola Casarini, Antonio Fiori, Nam-Kook Kim and Jea-Seung Lee, and Ramon Pacheco Pardo (eds.) *The Routledge Handbook of Europe-Korea Relations* (London: Routledge, 2021).

33 Jolyon Howorth, "EU Global Strategy in a changing world: Brussels' approach to the emerging powers." *Contemporary Security Policy* 37, no. 3 (2016): 391.

34 Paul Cornish and Geoffrey Edwards, "The strategic culture of the European Union: a progress report", *International Affairs* 81, no. 4 (2005): 802.

35 Ramon P. Pardo, Linde Desmaele, and Maximilian Ernst, "EU-ROK relations putting the strategic partnership to work," 5.

36 Carmen-Cristina Cîrlig, "EU Strategic Partnerships with Third Countries," Library Briefing, Library of the European Parliament, published September 26 2012, 5, https://www.europarl.europa.eu/RegData/bibliotheque/briefing/2012/120354/LDM_BRI(2012)120354_REV1_EN.pdf. (accessed 29 November 2021).

37 For ethical power, see Lisbeth Aggestam, "Introduction: ethical power Europe," *International Affairs* 84, no. 1 (2008): 1-11.

38 Ian Manners, "The Normative ethics of the European Union," *International Affairs* 84, No. 1 (2008): 57-58.

Bibliography

Aggestam, Lisbeth. "Introduction: ethical power Europe." International Affairs 84, no. 1 (2008): 1-11.

Aoki, Naoko. "KEDO: How multilateral cooperation helped an unprecedented North Korean project." CISSM Working Paper, September 2017.

Buzan, Barry, Ole Weaver and Jaap de Wilde. Security: A new framework for analysis. Boulder: Lynne Rienner Publishers, 1998.

Cîrlig, Carmen-Cristina. "EU Strategic Partnerships with Third Countries." Library Briefing, Library of the European Parliament, 26, September 26 2012. Available at https://www.europarl.europa.eu/RegData/bibliotheque/briefing/2012/120354/LDM_BRI(2012)120354_REV1_EN.pdf.

Cornish, Paul and Geoffrey Edwards. "The strategic culture of the European Union: a progress report." *International Affairs* 81, no. 4 (2005): 801-820.

Deutsch, W Karl. Political Community and the North Atlantic Area. International Organization in the Light of Historical Experience. Princeton, NJ: Princeton University Press, 1957.

Diez, Thomas. "Constructing the Self and Changing Others. Reconsidering `Normative Power Europe'." Millennium: Journal of International Studies 33, no.3 (2005): 613-636.

Diez, Thomas and Nathalie Tocci, The EU, Promoting Regional Integration, and Conflict Resolution (eds.). Basingstoke: Palgrave Macmillan, 2017.

European Commission. "Toward a New Asia Strategy. COM (94) 314 final." European Commission, 13, July 13 1994, Brussels, Available at https://eur-lex.europa.eu/legal-content/EN/TXT/PDF/?uri=CELEX:51994DC0314&from=EN.

Falk, Richard., "A 'New Medievalism'?." In Greg Fry and Jacinta O'Hagan (eds.),

Contending Images of World Politics. London and New York: Routledge, 2000.

Higashino, Atsuko. "For the Sake of 'Peace and Security'? The Role of Security in the European Union Enlargement Eastwards." Cooperation and Conflict 39, no. 4 (2004): 347-368.

Holsti, K. J.. "National Role Conceptions in the Study of Foreign Policy." International Studies Quarterly 14, no. 3 (1970): 233-309.

Howorth, Jolyon. "EU Global Strategy in a changing world: Brussels' approach to the emerging powers." Contemporary Security Policy 37, no. 3 (2016): 389-401.

Jun, Hae-won, "EU-ROK in Crisis Management Operations." In Nicola Casarini, Antonio Fiori, Nam-Kook Kim and Jea-Seung Lee, and Ramon Pacheco Pardo (eds.), The

Routledge Handbook of Europe-Korea Relations. London: Routledge, 2021.
Kartman, Charles, Robert Carlin and Joel Wit. "Policy in Context: A History of KEDO 1994-2006." June 2012. Standford: CISAC, 2012.
Manners, Ian. 'Normative power Europe: a contradiction in terms?." Journal of Common Market Studies 40, no. 2 (2002): 235-258.
Manners, Ian. "The Normative ethics of the European Union." International Affairs 84, no. 1 (2008): 45-60.
Michalski, Anna and Zhongqi Pan. "Role Dynamics in a Structural Relationship: The EU-China Strategic Partnership." Journal of Common Market Studies 55, no. 3 (2017): 611-627.
Mitrany, David. "The prospect of integration: Federal or functional." Journal of Common Market Studies 4, no. 2 (1965): 119-149.
Mitzen, Jennifer. "Anchoring Europe's civilizing identity: habits, capabilities and ontological security." Journal of European Public Policy 13, no. 2 (2006): 270-285.
Lee, Moosung. "The EU, regional cooperation, and the North Korean nuclear crisis." Asia Europe Journal 14, no. 4 (2016): 401-415.
Lee, Moosung and Thomas Diez. "Introduction: the EU, East Asian conflicts, and the norm of integration." Asia Europe Journal 14, no. 4 (2016): 353-366.
Lee, Moosung. "The EU and Six-Party Talks." In Casarini Nicola (ed.), Promoting Security Cooperation and Trust Building in Northeast Asia: The Role of the European Union. Roma: Nuova Cultura, 2017.
Pardo, P. Ramon, Linde Desmaele, and Maximilian Ernst. "EU-ROK relations putting the strategic partnership to work." KF-VUB KOREA Chair Report. October, 2018. Available at https://www.ies.be/files/EU-ROK_RELATIONS.pdf.
Rosamond, Ben. "The uniting of Europe and the foundation of EU studies: revisiting the neofunctionalism of Ernst B. Haas." European Journal of Public Policy 12, no. 2 (2005): 237-254.
Smith, Michael and Huaxian Xie. "The European Union and China" The Logics of 'Strategic Partnership."' Journal of Contemporary European Research 6, no. 4 (2010): 432-448.
Vahl, Marisu. "Just good friends? The EU-Russian 'Strategic Partnership' and the Northern Dimension." CEPS Working Document, no. 166, March 2001.
Waltz, Kenneth. Theory of International Politics. London: Addison-Wesley Pubishng Company, 1979.
Wendt, Alexander. Social Theory of International Politics. Cambridge: Cambridge University Press, 1997.
Wiessala, Georg. Re-Orienting the Fundaments: Human Rights and New Connections in EU-Asia Relations. Aldershot, Ashgate, 2006.

Europe in the Indo-Pacific – It's a Start

Axel Berkofsky

Introduction

This chapter examines the quality, impact and the (arguably many) shortcomings of recently published EU and European Indo-Pacific policy papers and strategies. The European and EU Indo-Pacific policy papers and strategies published from 2018 until today look ambitious on paper and are aimed at spelling out substantive and sustainable European contributions to security and stability in the Indo-Pacific region. However, it remains yet to be seen whether the EU will be able to turn rhetoric into action any time soon or ever. Regardless of whether (or rather whether not) European Indo-Pacific policy papers will stand for the 'big bang' of a European role in and impact on security in the Indo-Pacific, there is no doubt that European and EU Indo-Pacific policy papers have primarily been written and published against the background of very assertive and indeed increasingly aggressive Chinese policies such as China building military bases on artificially-built islets close to disputed islands in the South China Sea, Chinese unlawful intrusions into Japanese-controlled territorial waters in the East China Sea and the disturbingly frequent intrusion of Chinese fighter jets into Taiwanese-controlled airspace.

The Indo-Pacific region is comprised of the Indian and Pacific Oceans and is home to more than 30 percent of the global population. Half of the world's maritime trade, close to 50 percent of container traffic and 70 percent of global oil and gas travel through the Indian Ocean region. More than 40 percent of the world's offshore petroleum and mineral deposits are located in the Indian Ocean.[1] When Tokyo talks about 'free and open access' to international waters in the context of its 'Free and Open Indo-Pacific' (FOIP) policy, it means unrestricted access to maritime routes in the Indo-Pacific in the case of (Chinese) attempts to limit and/or block free passage through the sea lines of communication in the Indo-Pacific. The kind of 'free and open' access guaranteed by the kind of cooperation and coordination practised in the framework of the Quadrilateral Security Dialogue (Quad) initiated by then Japanese Prime Minister Shinzo Abe in 2007.[2] Germany and the Netherlands published their Indo-Pacific policy guidelines in 2020.[3] France adopted its Indo-Pacific strategy already in 2018, while Britain followed suit in March 2021.[4] Britain is not a newcomer to the Indian Ocean region. Since April 2018 Britain has maintained a naval support facility in Bahrain, in addition to what are referred to as its six 'permanent points of presence' in the Indian Ocean: Oman, Kenya, Brunei, Singapore, Diego Garcia and Qatar.[5]

Finally, the European Union (EU) published its Indo-Pacific policy guidelines in April and September 2021. All of this took place against the background of intensifying geopolitical competition and rivalry in the Indo-Pacific Region, with China at the centre of many of the region's conflicts. Indeed, there is (very) little doubt that Beijing building civilian facilities and military bases on artificial geographical features around and close to disputed islands in the South China Sea, challenging Japanese sovereignty over the Senkaku Islands in the East China Sea and the increasingly frequent presence of Chinese naval military forces in the Indian Ocean have motivated the EU in its IndoPacific policy papers issued in 2021 to announce what it calls an 'increased naval presence' in the Indo-Pacific.[6] However, Brussels has yet to add the details of what this 'increased naval presence' it first mentioned in April 2021 will eventually result in: a semi-permanent or indeed permanent European naval presence in the East and/or South China Seas or instead occasional (but increasingly frequent) deployments of European naval forces to the Indo-Pacific? The EU's Indo-Pacific strategy paper mentions a number of issues and areas which Brussels will be more involved in. However, like it is very often the case with EU policy or strategy papers, without mentioning many details explaining what exactly Brussels wants to do when and with whom in the Indo-Pacific. Policymakers in Brussels and EU Member State capitals confirm, albeit still and more often than not off the record[7], that there is an increasing European interest in making a contribution to stability and security in the Indo-Pacific due to increasing Chinese assertiveness accompanied by successful Chinese attempts to tip the territorial status quo in the South China Sea in its favour. Such increased interest dates back to 2018 when the EU Council issued its Asia policy paper entitled 'Enhanced EU Security Cooperation in and with Asia' –a comprehensive and detailed policy paper listing numerous areas and issues on which Brussels is planning to intensify cooperation with a number of East, Southeast and South Asian countries.[8] To state that Beijing is 'unhappy' about an increased European interest and presence in the Indo-Pacific in general and the envisioned 'meaningful naval presence' is an understatement. China's 'wolf-warrior diplomats' use Twitter and editorials in Chinese state-controlled and state-censored newspapers[9] to express their anger about Europe's plans to make more tangible contributions to security in the Indo-Pacific[10]. This is done through the sort of aggressive rhetoric and threats that seem to have convinced European policymakers that observing (for now mostly from a safe distance) Chinese expansionist territorial policies in the South China Sea, Chinese unlawful interference in Hong Kong's political and judicial affairs, Beijing oppressing and detaining Chinese citizens of Muslim faith in the Chinese province of Xinjiang and increasingly frequently intrusions into Taiwan's Air Defence Identification Zone (ADIZ)[11], should no longer be an option. Indeed, Europe seems to be prepared to act on the conclusion that issuing declarations - alone or jointly with (for example Japan) - reminding Beijing to adhere to international law has not led to China reducing its territorial expansionism in the South China Sea. In fact, quite the opposite has been the case in recent years. Verbally protesting against Chinese territorial expansionism did not and continues not to mean that Beijing has not continued to build military bases on artificially built islands close to disputed islands in the South China Sea. Quite the opposite is the case: satellite footage shows that Beijing has instead accelerated the construction of military facilities over recent years. A report by the geospatial software company *Simularity* published in February 2021 revealed what is most probably infrastructure for radar and antennae as part of a military base on the Mischief Reef. The Mischief is a ring-shaped coral reef located roughly 250 kilometres away from the Philippines and has been occupied by China since 1995. This is the kind of reef that China cannot legitimately claim as part of its territory as stipulated by the Permanent Court of Arbitration (PCA) in 2016. The PCA ruled that the Mischief Reef is located within the Exclusive Economic Zone (EEZ) of the Philippines and therefore cannot be claimed by China.[12] Other satellite pictures taken in March 2021 show that China has reclaimed land to extend Subi Reef in and around the Spratly Islands in the South China Sea. Photos taken by the space technology company Maxar show the land added to Subi Reef, which is claimed by Vietnam and the Philippines.[13] Furthermore, since 2014 China has transformed a number of reefs and sandbars – often very far from its own shoreline – into man-made artificial islands fortified with missiles, runways and various weapons systems. In the Spratly archipelago, which is claimed by Brunei, China, Malaysia, the Philippines, Taiwan and Vietnam, Beijing has built 13 square kilometres of artificial islands on top of reefs and rocks (on which it has deployed missiles).

Outside the EU, Western democracies are joining forces to seek to pressurise China into respecting and abiding by international law and verdicts on who can and cannot claim land and maritime territory in the Indo-Pacific. In September 2020 the UK, Germany and France jointly submitted a *Note Verbale* to the United Nations (UN) urging Beijing to respect a verdict pronounced by The Hague-based Permanent Court of Arbitration (PCA) in 2016. In a case brought forward by the Philippines, the court had ruled that China's historic territorial claims in the South China Sea were unlawful, obsolete and in non-compliance with international law as stipulated in the United Nations Convention on the Law of the Sea (UNCLOS)[14] which China has ratified.

Sailing to the Indian Ocean

Roughly 35 percent of the EU 27's export go to the Indo-Pacific. 90 percent of those goods pass through the Indian and Pacific Oceans.[15] Europe and the U.S. under President Joe Biden agree on who is the elephant in the room and nowadays there is very little – if any – talk of engaging China politically. For their part, European countries have found that China really is the kind of 'systemic rival' Brussels calls the country since March 2019: an authoritarian country whose approaches to international politics and security are so fundamentally different from EU approaches that cooperation in international politics and security has turned out to be an illusion more than anything else. Certainly, policymakers in EU Member States continue to reserve the right to decide – typically without consulting EU policymakers and institutions – the extent to which they are prepared to mention China in the context of a 'systemic rivalry.' The UK and France are envisioning concrete security cooperation on the ground with Washington, Tokyo, New Delhi and Canberra in the framework of the aforementioned Quad. In April 2021, for example, the four Quad countries – the US, India, Australia and Japan – joined a France-led naval drill in the Bay of Bengal.[16] The French La Perouse[17] exercise was first conducted in 2019 and is part of what is referred to as 'Quad Plus' exercises. Pankaj Jha, the former deputy director of India's National Security Council Secretariat and today professor of defence and strategic studies at O.P. Jindal Global University, argues that France increasing its naval engagement with the Quad is also a reaction to China searching for mineral resources in waters around French territories in the Indian Ocean. "France has been aware of the fact that the Chinese have been making certain under sea moves [scavenging for minerals and resources], particularly in French territories in the Indian Ocean, so they wanted to do something that acts as a deterrent and also as a collaborative effort," he is cited as saying in an interview with the paper Nikkei Asia.[18] Furthermore, British defence planners are envisioning to intensify naval coordination and collaboration with India and Japan as part of what is referred to as 'mini-laterals' between like-minded countries in the Indo-

Pacific region. This as part of the UK's so-called 'tilt' to the Indo-Pacific announced in 2021.[19]

If it Looks like a Duck…

While Beijing might interpret Paris and London joining the Quad countries conducting military exercises in the Indo-Pacific as European countries (and the EU) inevitably joining US-driven China containment policies, conducting military manoeuvres among like-minded democracies protecting their common economic and security interests is not unusual. This is especially the case when there is a consensus that that their economic and security interests must be defended against the ambitions of one country. This is where clarity and political courage should be injected into the discourse: China constantly complains about[20] containment directed against itself while refusing to accept (but undoubtedly understanding) that Quad military exercises would not take place if it were not for Chinese aggressive continuous territorial expansionism. The aforementioned satellite pictures made public by European Space Imaging in March 2018 provide unambiguous evidence toward that end.[21] Furthermore, Beijing continues to challenge Japanese sovereignty over Japanese-controlled Senkaku Islands in the East China Sea[22] and its naval forces are sailing increasingly frequently into the Indian Ocean. China is expanding economic and military relations with countries such as India's arch-enemy Pakistan and with recipients of large-scale Chinese investments such as Sri Lanka and Bangladesh. Of course, none of this comes for free. Sri Lanka e.g. owes China more money than it will ever be able to repay. This is how Beijing was able to pressure Sri Lanka into granting China territorial concessions in return for debt reduction: Chinese so-called 'debt trap' diplomacy, which is bound to intensify the more China invests in developing countries in need of cash and investments.[23]

France's Indo-Pacific Strategy

France's Indo-Pacific strategy was first published in 2018.[24] The self-proclaimed 'resident power,' is determined to defend French territorial rights and sovereignty in the region: the islands of Mayotte and La Réunion, the Scattered island and the French Southern and Antarctic Territories in the southern part of the Indian Ocean. Furthermore, France has territories in New Caledonia, Wallis and Futuna, French Polynesia and Clipperton Island. 1.6 million French citizens live in the Indo-Pacific Region and about 8.000 French troops are permanently based there. Although the 8.000 French troops can probably not be deemed a 'massive' military presence in the Indo-Pacific region, they are very well equipped. In the United Arab Emirates (UAE) and Djibouti, Paris has deployed six Rafale fighter jets and four Mirage-2.000 fighters respectively. In the southern Indian Ocean French troops are stationed on La Réunion and Mayotte island and they operate two surveillance frigates, a supply and support vessel, two patrol vessels and two tactical transport aircraft. In the Pacific Ocean, French troops are stationed in New Caledonia and French Polynesia, operating two surveillance frigates, each equipped with a helicopter, three patrol vessels, two multi-mission ships, five maritime surveillance aircraft and four tactical transport aircraft. Furthermore, Paris has 18 resident and non-resident defence attachés stationed in 33 countries in the Indo-Pacific Region. Finally, France is working with the regional centres charged with the surveillance of maritime spaces and sea lines of communication in the region. France has deployed three naval officers to the Information Fusion Center of Singapore (IFC), the Regional Centre for the Fusion of Maritime Information (CRFIM) in Madagascar and the Information Fusion Center, Indian Ocean Region (IFC-IOR) located in New Delhi. In September 2019, French President Macron positioned France as a 'balancing power' in the Indo-Pacific. However, Paris has yet to explain how exactly and by which concrete means France is planning to become a 'balancing power' in the Indo-Pacific. Cooperation with the U.S. navy such as joint patrolling in territorial waters in the Indo-Pacific bilaterally or in the framework of the Quad could be part of the envisioned balancing power policies. The French Ministry of Defence identifies access to deep water resources, the expansion of military power projection capabilities, anti-access/area denial capabilities and advances in cyberspace and satellite capabilities as challenges Paris needs to meet in order to be able to compete with China in the region.[25] To address these issues, Paris has announced to expand the country's security ties with Australia, India, Japan, Malaysia, New Zealand, Indonesia and Vietnam.

Germany's Indo-Pacific Guidelines
Not the Big Bang of German Involvement in the Indo-Pacific

Germany's Indo-Pacific policy guidelines released in 2020 are not – to put it bluntly – the breakthrough of tangible and measurable German contributions to security in the Indo-Pacific.[26] The guidelines deal with increased German security engagement in the region through port calls, joint exercises and protection of global maritime trade routes. Furthermore, the guidelines talk about a 'diversification of its partnerships in the region beyond China.' This statement sounds awkward, as in reality there are no German political and security ties with China that could be referred to as 'partnerships.' Instead, Germany's engagement with China is above all aimed at facilitating the expansion of trade and business ties of German companies and investors with Chinese counterparts.[27] Moving beyond diplomatic wishful thinking and formulas which do not describe the reality of the security environment in the Indo-Pacific, Germany's political and security 'partnerships' in Asia/the Indo-Pacific Region exist with fellow democracies in the region, such as Japan, Australia, India and South Korea.

Furthermore, more than 60 times the German guidelines mention the Indo-Pacific as an 'ASEAN-centric' security architecture. This is despite the fact that ASEAN's role in and actual impact on (hard) security issues and (existing and potential) security conflicts in the Indo-Pacific is arguably very limited at best. ASEAN – often under pressure from China – typically cites the 'principle of non-interference' when it chooses not to criticise Chinese territorial expansionist policies openly in a straightforward manner. Chinese threats of economic retaliation have proven efficient at keeping Southeast Asian countries (which count and indeed depend on Chinese investments) from becoming too outspoken about Beijing building military bases on or close to islands that are subject to territorial disputes between China and themselves. This is hardly the kind of 'ASEAN-centred' security environment Germany's Indo-Pacific guidelines claim to have identified. ASEAN's security forum, the ASEAN Regional Forum (ARF), does not get sustainably involved in, let alone resolve, security conflicts in the region in general and territorial disputes in particular. Since it was established in 1994, the ARF[28] has been an informal gathering of foreign ministers, not equipped with the authority or instruments to make legally binding decisions.

Berlin seems to have concluded that the elusive code of conduct between China and ASEAN on territorial disputes can resolve tensions and territorial disputes in the South China Sea, the scholar Andreas Fulda writes.[29] In reality, negotiations on the China-ASEAN Code of Conduct (COC) for the South China Sea have not made any progress at all and it indeed seems very unlikely that the code could be adopted any time soon, if at all.[30] Moreover, such a code has now de facto become obsolete as China is occupying the very islands in the South China Sea it has committed itself to negotiate on with ASEAN since 2002. Finally, the code will not be signed because China continues to categorically reject UNCLOS provisions on the South China Sea, obviously because these provisions – as it was the case in 2016 when an arbitration panel ruled that China's historical territorial claims in the South China Sea were in non-compliance with international law and therefore do not confirm China's territorial claims. For their part, ASEAN members will not meet China's requests to not conduct military exercises with outside parties as a precondition for Beijing signing this code of conduct. Almost needless to say that the Quad countries in general and the U.S. in particular are meant by 'outside parties.'[31]

Finally, the German guidelines talk about the involvement of

NATO in security in the Indo-Pacific through cooperation with Japan and South Korea (both are NATO dialogue partners belonging to a group of countries which are referred to as 'partners across the globe'[32]). However, no details are given as to how Japan and South Korea would or could contribute to NATO's (possible) involvement in security in the Indo-Pacific. The guidelines furthermore refer to a proposed partnership with India (India is mentioned 57 times in the document). Cooperation on non-traditional security issues, such as climate change, environmental security and public health is mentioned in this context. Andreas Fulda indicates what Berlin does not mention in its guidelines: China's disinformation campaigns on social media and Taiwan. The guidelines merely mention disinformation spread by 'authoritarian states,' despite the fact that there is ample evidence of Chinese disinformation campaigns, Fulda argues. Not mentioning Taiwan in the guidelines, means that Berlin is succumbing to China's insistence that Taiwan is not an autonomous/independent country but merely a renegade Chinese province. Referring to Taiwan as a Chinese 'province' in 2022 is – putting it bluntly – arguably all but completely nonsensical and sounds plausible in Chinese policymaking circles and there only.

Berlin Setting Sail & Teaming up with Tokyo

In November 2019, Berlin decided to set sail to the Pacific Ocean. It announced the deployment of a naval frigate to the Indian Ocean in 2020, including transit through the South China Sea.[33] The global pandemic, however, prevented the deployment at the time. In March of 2021 Berlin announced that the vessel would be deployed in the Indo-Pacific Region in August 2021 and would return to Germany six months later.[34] The German frigate will also sail towards the Korean Peninsula to join a multinational mission monitoring the United Nations sanctions regime imposed on North Korea. On its way back to Europe, the German naval vessel will also sail through the South China Sea, albeit not within 12 nautical miles of Chinese-claimed territories in the region, as the German government was quick to point out at the time. According to the United Nations Convention on the Law of the Seas (UNCLOS), every state has the right to establish what UNCLOS defines as 'territorial sea' to the extent of 12 nautical miles.[35] Within this zone, coastal states exercise sovereignty over the air space above the sea, the seabed and the subsoil. By announcing it would not sail within 12 nautical miles of Chinese-claimed disputed islands in the South China Sea, Berlin is giving the impression to have de facto recognised Beijing's unlawful territorial claims in the South China Sea. Otherwise, the German frigate could or would sail into Beijing's self-declared 12 nautical mile zone, not recognising it as such but instead as international waters. This in turn would confirm that Berlin does not recognise China's territorial claims in the South China Sea in accordance with the 2016 verdict by the Permanent Court of Arbitration. Berlin, however, has decided against challenging Chinese unlawful territorial claims in the South China Sea. All of this unfortunately means that the German naval operation in the South China Sea has become a potentially counterproductive exercise as it de facto recognises Chinese territorial sovereignty over disputed islands. In the past the U.S. navy has conducted so-called 'Freedom of Navigation Operations' (FONOPs) in the South China Sea, challenging (since 2016 officially unlawful) Chinese territorial claims there. This entailed U.S. navy vessels sailing within 12 nautical miles of Chinese-claimed islands. Beijing of course protested every time this happened, which is most probably the reason why the German navy has ruled out conducting similar FONOPs in the South China Sea. Instead, it has decided that its frigate will navigate on a zig-zag course around the Chinese-defined 12 nautical mile zone. In fairness, the U.S. is currently the only country conducting FONOPs in the South China Sea within what China insists is its 12 nautical mile zone. Washington's Asian allies and fellow Quad countries, Japan, India and Australia, have so far been reluctant to join U.S.- led FONOPs.[36] This does not mean that only the U.S. navy is patrolling the South China Sea. Among others in 2021a French submarine has been patrolling the South China Sea and British naval forces, including a new aircraft carrier, are expected to do their share of patrolling there in the months ahead. Berlin, on the other hand, by explicitly and a priori reassuring China that it is adjusting its course in the South China Sea according to Chinese illegal territorial claims, has made an announcement devoid of political courage or common sense – a declaration from a government determined to do (almost) everything possible to make sure that its navy's passage through the South China Sea goes as unnoticed as possible in Beijing. However, the past has shown that foreign vessels sailing through the South China Sea have typically led to Chinese protests and accusations of violating alleged Chinese national territory.

There were German concerns beyond the South China Sea. Michito Tsuruoka and Hans Kundnani cite the concerns of German officials in a May 2021 Chatham House commentary that a scheduled port visit of the German frigate to Shanghai could convey the impression that Berlin had previously asked Beijing for permission to enter the South China Sea.[37] Tsuruoka and Kundnani suggest, Beijing would indeed not have granted the German frigate Bayern to stop in Shanghai if the frigate had sailed into the South China Sea against China's will. Tsuruoka and Kundnani conclude that the modified German deployment plan makes encounters between German and other European naval forces deployed in the Indo-Pacific unlikely or even impossible. According to the original planning Germany's frigate could have joined three overlapping deployments in the region: the British carrier strike group led by HMS Queen Elizabeth II, a Dutch frigate and the French Mistral-class amphibious assault ship Tonnerre. These encounters could not take place as the German frigate sailed anti-clockwise through the Indian Ocean. "So, rather than coordinating with European allies, let alone the United States, Germany is doing its own thing – a missed opportunity," according to a German official quoted by Tsuruoka and Kundnani. All these manoeuvres turned out to be irrelevant when Beijing in mid-September decided not to allow the German naval vessel to call the port of Shanghai for a stopover. [38] In fact, not a surprise it was always very unlikely that the Chinese authorities would allow a German vessel sailing into the South China Sea to call the port of Shanghai. The German Ministry of Defence announcing in the wake of the vessel's departure towards the Indo-Pacific that the port call in Shanghai would strengthen the dialogue between Berlin and Beijing always sounded very awkward and lacked any credibility. But that did not matter either as Beijing was never interested in giving the 'middle power' Germany with its second-tier navy a platform to present its cruise into the Indo-Pacific as a policy resulting in increased dialogue with China.

Germany and Japan

In early April 2021 Tokyo and Berlin announced they would hold their first 2+2 discussions on security in the Indo-Pacific (a meeting of the German and Japanese defence and foreign ministers).[39] Nikkei Asia at the time was quick to identify a shift in German foreign and security policies towards China, accompanied by increased German on-the-ground contributions to security in the Indo-Pacific.[40] However, discussing security in the Indo-Pacific with Tokyo is relevant and constructive but it does not mean that the talks will lead to German and Japanese navies jointly policing Chinese intrusions in the East China Sea, something Tokyo has wanted European countries and their navies to do for some time. If the German navy joined the Japanese navy patrolling in the East China Sea, the symbolic German contribution to security in the Indo-Pacific would indeed become a very concrete one. However, there are obstacles standing in the way of such a German contribution. Sailing towards and through the South China Sea calling it 'innocent' passage is one thing. It is quite another to jointly patrol the East China Sea alongside Japan's navy – from a Chinese perspective undoubtedly it would be the ultimate evidence that Germany had signed up to U.S.-Japanese China containment policies, the sort of corner Germany does not want to find itself in.

The question remains where the limits are as regards Western tolerance towards Chinese regional territorial expansionism. In other words, how many more military bases is Beijing allowed to build on disputed islands in the South China Sea, how many times will Chinese unlawful intrusions into Taiwanese airspace and Japanese territorial waters be tolerated before Beijing is confronted with a robust Western reaction that goes beyond verbally protesting against Beijing's policies to no avail? How many more times will allied Western countries stand idly by when Beijing imposes economic blackmail policies and sanctions onto countries like the Philippines, Mongolia, Australia, Canada and others before responding to Chinese sanctions with political and economic sanctions that have the potential to hurt Chinese political and more importantly economic interests? These are questions that will have to be addressed more seriously and in a more concerted and multilateral manner, unless Beijing fundamentally changes the quality of its currently aggressive regional security policies 'voluntarily' (which is very unlikely).

The EU's Indo-Pacific Policy Strategy (September 2021)

On 16 April 2021, the Council of the European Union issued its 'Conclusions on an EU Strategy for Cooperation in the Indo-Pacific.'[41] In September the EU Commission published 'The EU Strategy for Cooperation in the Indo-Pacific.'[42] The EU announced what it called a "meaningful European naval presence in the Indo-Pacific." However, the exact meaning of this phrase and who and what would be deployed to the region has yet to emerge. Certainly, the expression "a meaningful presence" paired with "EU strategic autonomy in Asia" in the EU policy paper signals a new approach by policymakers in Brussels. In the EU's defence, the Indo-Pacific policy strategy published in 2021 is more concrete and tangible than many previous EU Asia policy papers. This will be noticed by policymakers in Beijing and they of course understand that China is targeted even if not named. Indeed, the EU's guidelines make it very clear to the reader that Beijing's policies are the core of what Brussels is concerned about as regards stability in the Indo-Pacific. They state "the Council notes however with concern the current dynamics in the Indo-Pacific that have given rise to intense geopolitical competition adding to increasing tensions on trade and supply chains as well as in technological, political and security areas. The universality of human rights is also being challenged." Without any doubt China and its policies are in the focus when the guidelines address both "geopolitical competition and tensions" and the challenge to the "universality of human rights." The guidelines furthermore state that the "EU will deepen its engagement on the Indo-Pacific in particular with those partners that have already announced Indo-Pacific approaches of their own."

The EU strategy also announces that the "EU will further develop partnerships and strengthen synergies with like-minded partners and relevant organisations in security and defence. This will include responding to challenges to international security, including maritime security, malicious cyber activities, disinformation, as well as from emerging and disruptive technologies, countering and improving resilience to terrorism, violent extremism and hybrid threats, countering organised crime and illicit trafficking, in full compliance with international law." Again, China is the central protagonist: provider of disruptive technologies, disinformation campaigns, author of threats to maritime security etc. From a realpolitik point of view, however, China should have been named in the EU's Indo-Pacific strategy, as there is ample evidence that Beijing continues to be behind a number of cyber-attacks. Next to Russia China is the most active disinformation campaign protagonist in the region and globally.

Finally, the EU's Indo-Pacific strategy envisions cooperation between Europe and other countries in the region in the framework of EU Common Security and Defence Policy missions (CSDP). However, the EU does not cite any examples and/or scenarios where and how such cooperation can be realised. In reality, such cooperation is much easier said than actually done on the ground. Japan and the EU, for example, have sought for years unsuccessfully to institutionalise Japanese contributions to EU CSDP missions. While Japanese troops have in the past contributed to CSDP missions in Africa and Central Asia, that took place on an ad-hoc basis without an institutional framework basis. The guidelines also talk about increased EU contributions to the ARF. However, neither ASEAN nor ARF are equipped with the authority and instruments to make legally binding decisions relevant to hard/traditional security in the Indo-Pacific.

Conclusions

Beijing changing the territorial status quo on land and sea in parts of the Indo-Pacific and deciding that Chinese-drawn maps authorise it to unilaterally claim territory has led to a pooling of naval and military forces among like-minded countries. No doubt this is part of a China containment strategy in the Indo-Pacific against the background of Chinese territorial ambitions which might one day go (far) beyond building military bases on the disputed islands in the South China Sea. As London School of Economics China scholar William Callahan has documented in his book *China Dreams: 20 Visions of the Future,* China has a plan to reincorporate much of the rest of Asia into a new Chinese empire.[43]

Europe's and European attempts and aspirations to engage China politically and get Beijing to respect and implement international law have not worked. If Europe's goal is to deter China from treating disputed waters and territories as their own and building military runways on them, time will tell whether the EU, French and German Indo-Pacific policy strategies have contributed to this end. The options available to Europe (and the U.S. for that matter) to keep Beijing from building military bases on disputed islands are limited and have the potential to lead to armed conflict. Blocking Chinese access to disputed islands in the South China Sea through a sea blockade with the U.S. for example would undoubtedly be interpreted as an act of war by Beijing. Although such a blockade is not openly discussed among countries within and outside the region, it is undoubtedly discussed among like-minded and allied countries such as the Quad members. The self-proclaimed regional 'resident power' France approaches security in the Indo-Pacific differently from Germany. While Germany will continue to have the luxury of focussing on its trade and investment ties in the Indo-Pacific, Paris needs to protect those 1.6 million plus French citizens permanently living in the region. Against this background, the French Indo-Pacific policy guidelines are tangible and give readers a good understanding of what France and its naval forces are planning to do in the region in the years ahead.

The German Indo-Pacific policy guidelines on the other hand are far less tangible, not allowing the reader to understand how and to what extent they represent a new German approach to the region. Putting ASEAN at the centre of German efforts to contribute to security in the Indo-Pacific is a case in point. Berlin's deployment of a frigate to the Indo-Pacific region in 2021 is welcome, despite its mere symbolic nature. It may be too symbolic and not substantive and credible enough for the world's fourth largest economy and Asia's biggest European trading and investment partner. Berlin omitting to mention Taiwan in its Indo-Pacific policy guidelines looks like a conscious decision to not offend Beijing and avoid of being accused of interfering in China's internal affairs. From a regional security point of view this is lacking credibility. Policymakers in Beijing can hence conclude that there is no reason to worry about any German interference in China's alleged internal affairs.

---

1 See, e.g., Timothy Doyle, *Blue Economy and the Ocean Rim*, Journal of the Indian Ocean Region, Vol. 14, 2018, pp. 1-6; Iyer, Gayathri, Mega-ships in the Indian Ocean: Evaluating the Impact and Exploring Littoral Cooperation, ORF Occasional Paper No. 204, Observer Research Foundation July 2019, https://www.orfonline.org/research/mega-ships-in-the-indian-ocean-evaluating-the-impact-and-exploring-littoral-cooperation-53235/.

2 For further details, see, e.g., Patrick Gerard Buchan, Benjamin Rimland, *Defining the Diamond: The Past, Present, and Future of the Quadrilateral Security Dialogue*, CSIS Brief, Center for Strategic and International Studies (CSIS) March 16, 2020, https://www.csis.org/analysis/defining-diamond-past-present-and-future-quadrilateral-security-dialogue.

3 The German guidelines are called 'Policy Guidelines for the Indo-Pacific.' The Dutch guidelines are called: 'Indo-Pacific: Guidelines for Strengthening Dutch and EU Cooperation with Partners in Asia.'

4 For the details of Britain's policies in and towards the Indo-Pacific, see Global Britain in a Competitive Age. The Integrated Review of Security, Defence, Development and Foreign Policy March 2021, https://www.gov.uk/government/publications/global-britain-in-a-competitive-age-the-integrated-review-of-security-defence-development-and-foreign-policy/global-britain-in-a-competitive-age-the-integrated-review-of-security-defence-development-and-foreign-policy.

5 For further details see Rahul-Roy Chaudhury, *Understanding the UK's Tilt Towards the Indo-Pacific*, Chatham House Commentary April 15, 2021, https://www.iiss.org/blogs/analysis/2021/04/uk-indo-pacific-tilt.

6 For details see also Coordinated Maritime Presences: Council extends in the Gulf of Guinea for two years and establishes a new Maritime Area of Interest in he North-Western Indian Ocean, Council of the European Union February 21, 2022, https://www.consilium.europa.eu/en/press/press-releases/2022/02/21/coordinated-maritime-presences-council-extends-implementation-in-the-gulf-of-guinea-for-2-years-and-establishes-a-new-concept-in-the-north-west-indian-ocean/

7 In conversations with this author in 2020 and 2021.

8 See Enhanced EU Security Cooperation in and with Asia, Council of the European Union, Brussels May 28, 2018, https://www.consilium.europa.eu/media/35456/st09265-re01-en18.pdf.

9 In essence all of China's newspapers.

10 Chinese 'wolf-warrior' diplomacy makes reference to a very popular Chinese action movie series in which Chinese soldiers and fighters easily and gloriously defeat China's adversaries and enemies. The language used in the Twitter accounts of China's Ministry of Foreign Affairs spokespersons in particular seems to have been inspired by the aforementioned Chinese (government-approved) action movie series, language and rhetoric aggressively defending China against accusations of all kinds via social media channels which are not accessible by ordinary Chinese citizens. Twitter is not accessible by the 'ordinary' Chinese citizen. See China's Wolf-Warrior Gamble. Foreign Policy is not like an Action Film, The Economist May 30, 2020. See also Rachel Cheung, and Benjamin Wilhelm, *Why China's 'Wolf-Warriors' Won't Back Down*, World Politics Review (WPR) April 7, 2021, https://www.worldpoliticsreview.com/trend-lines/29554/china-s-wolf-warrior-diplomacy-is-here-to-stay.

11 See e.g. Taiwan: Record Number of China Jets Enter Air Zone, BBC News April 13, 2021; https://www.bbc.com/news/world-asia-56728072.

12 See, e.g., South China Sea: Satellite Images Show China Building Full-Blown Military Bases on Artificial Islands, The New Zealand Herald, February 21, 2021, https://www.nzherald.co.nz/world/south-china-sea-satellite-images-show-china-building-full-blown-military-bases-on-artificial-islands/DAM22R4VYYCKYAZRPRION7ISXU/.

13 See Kristin Huang, *South China Sea: China has Extended another Spratly Islands Reef, Photos Show*, South China Morning Post March 24, 2021, https://www.scmp.com/news/china/military/article/3126656/south-china-sea-beijing-has-extended-another-spratly-islands.

14 See Christia Marie Ramos, *UK, France, Germany Refute China's Expansive South China Sea Claims*, Inquirer.Net September 18, 2020, https://globalnation.inquirer.net/190953/uk-france-germany-refute-chinas-expansive-south-china-sea-claims.

15 Garima Mohan, *A European Approach to the Indo-Pacific?*, Global Public Policy Institute August 20, 2020, https://www.gppi.net/2020/08/20/a-european-approach-to-the-indo-pacific.

16 See Kiran Sharma, and Mailys Penne-Lassus, *France to Lead Quad Naval Drill in Indo-Pacific Challenge to China*, Nikkei Asia April 2, 2021, https://asia.nikkei.com/Politics/International-relations/Indo-Pacific/France-to-lead-Quad-naval-drill-in-Indo-Pacific-challenge-to-China.

17 Named after an 18th century French explorer and naval officer.

18 Cited in Sharma, Penne-Lassus.

19 See, e.g., Duggal Mahima, *The Case for a Britain-India-Japan Trilateral*, Council on Geostrategy May 21, 2021, https://www.geostrategy.org.uk/britains-world/the-case-for-a-britain-india-japan-trilateral/.

20 By means of, e.g., the above-mentioned Chinese 'wolf-warriors.'

21 See Daniel Bishton, *Spratly Islands Military Bases Revealed Spatial Source*, March 6, 2018, https://spatialsource.com.au/satellite-images-reveal-completed-military-bases-spratly-islands/. The images show a deep water port, aerodromes, hangars, military barracks, communications infrastructure and a 2.7 km long runway on the Subi and Mischief reefs. See also James Griffith, *Beijing may have Built Bases in the South China Sea, but that doesn't mean it can Defend them, report claims*, CNN December 7, 2020, https://edition.cnn.com/2020/12/07/china/south-china-sea-bases-military-intl-hnk/index.html.

22 The Senkaku Islands have de facto been part of Japanese territory since the first Sino-Japanese War in 1894-1895. China claims that the islands (which are referred to as the Diaoyu Islands in China) have always been part of Chinese territory, while Tokyo maintains that they were 'terra nullius' when Tokyo annexed them in 1895. Because the Senkaku Islands were not part of the territories Japan was obliged render to China (or anybody else) with the adoption of the San Francisco Peace Treaty in 1951, Tokyo maintains that the islands continue to belong to Japan.

23 In 2017, in a 99-year lease the Sri Lankan Hambanthota Harbour was given to China Merchants Port Holding, a Chinese state-owned company. The Sri Lankan government granted the lease in order to reduce the debt it owed China deriving from previous loans. For details, see Maria Abi-Habib, *How China Got Sri Lanka to Cough up a Port*, New York Times June 28, 2018, https://www.nytimes.com/2018/06/25/world/asia/china-sri-lanka-port.html.

24 And updated in 2022, see France's Indo-Pacific Strategy, Gouvernement, https://www.diplomatie.gouv.fr/IMG/pdf/en_dcp_a4_indopacifique_022022_v1-4_web_cle878143.pdf

25 For details, see also France and Security in the Indo-Pacific, Ministère des Armes France, May 2019, https://www.defense.gouv.fr/layout/set/print/content/download/532754/9176250/version/3/file/France+and+Security+in+the+Indo-Pacific+-+2019.pdf.

26 See German-Europe-Asia. Shaping the 21st Century Together, Federal German Foreign Office, Berlin, August 2020, https://www.auswaertiges-amt.de/blob/2380514/f9784f7e3b3fa1bd7c5446d274a4169e/200901-indo-pazifik-leitlinien--1--data.pdf. For further details, see also Garima Mohan, *Germany Gets On Board With The Indo-Pacific*, 9DashLine, September 11, 2020; https://www.9dashline.com/article/germany-gets-on-board-the-indo-pacific and Singh, Gurjit, Germany Takes View of the Indo-Pacific, Observer Research Foundation (ORF), October 1, 2020, https://www.orfonline.org/expert-speak/germany-takes-view-indo-pacific/.

27 Certainly, Germany's efforts – similar to those of other European countries – are above all aimed at facilitating the creation of a level playing field for German companies investing in China, making sure that they can invest in business and industrial sectors as freely as Chinese companies can invest in Germany.

28 The ARF comprises 27 members: the 10 ASEAN member states (Brunei, Cambodia, Indonesia, Laos, Malaysia, Myanmar, Philippines, Singapore, Thailand and Vietnam), the 10 ASEAN dialogue partners (Australia, Canada, China, the European Union, India, Japan, New Zealand, the Republic of Korea, Russia and the United States), Bangladesh, North Korea, Mongolia, Pakistan, Sri Lanka, Timor-Leste and one ASEAN observer (Papua New Guinea).

29 See Andreas Fulda, *Germany's New Policy Paper for the Indo-Pacific: Some Change in Tone, Little in Substance*, RUSI Commentary, September 11, 2020; https://rusi.org/commentary/germanys-new-policy-paper-indo-pacific-some-change-tone-little-substance.

30 See, e.g., Viet Hoang, *The Code of Conduct for the South China Sea: A Long and Bumpy Road*, The Diplomat, September 28, 2020, https://thediplomat.com/2020/09/the-code-of-conduct-for-the-south-china-sea-a-long-and-bumpy-road/

31 See also In the South China Sea, America is Churning Waters Claimed by China, The Economist, July 25, 2020, https://www.economist.com/asia/2020/07/23/in-the-south-china-sea-america-is-

churning-waters-claimed-by-china.

32 Together with, e.g., Finland, Australia and New Zealand.

33 See Björn Müller, *Marine Plant die Entsendung einer Fregatte in den Indo-Pazifik*, Pivot Area, November 26, 2019, https://www.pivotarea.eu/2019/11/26/fregatte-in-den-indo-pazifik/.

34 See Johannes Leithäuser, *Deutschland Entsendet Fregatte in Ostasiatische Gewässer*, Frankfurter Allgemeine Zeitung, March 2, 2021, https://www.faz.net/aktuell/politik/inland/deutschland-entsendet-fregatte-in-indo-pazifik-raum-17224589.html.

35 According to UNCLOS, territorial sea extends to a limit of 12 nautical miles from the baseline of a coastal state.

36 The Quad is Finding its Purpose, at Last, The Economist, June 12, 2021, https://www.economist.com/asia/2021/06/12/the-quad-is-finding-its-purpose-at-last.

37 Michito Tsuruoka, and Hans Kundnani, *Germany's Indo-Pacific Frigate May Send Unclear Message*, Chatham House Expert Comment, May 4, 2021, https://www.chathamhouse.org/2021/05/germanys-indo-pacific-frigate-may-send-unclear-message.

38 See China Denies Port Visit by German Warship: Deutsche Welle (DW) September 15, 2021, https://www.dw.com/en/china-denies-port-visit-by-german-warship/a-59190643.

39 See Julian Ryall, *Japan, Germany's First 2 Plus 2 Shows Extent of Tokyo's Outreach Amid China's Rising Assertiveness: Analysts*, South China Morning Post, April 5, 2021; https://www.scmp.com/week-asia/politics/article/3128366/japan-germanys-first-2-plus-2-dialogue-shows-extent-tokyos .

40 See Takuya Mizorogi, *Japan Woos Germany on Indo-Pacific with first 2-Plus-2 Talks*, Nikkei Asia, April 6, 2021, https://asia.nikkei.com/Politics/International-relations/Japan-woos-Germany-on-Indo-Pacific-with-first-2-plus-2-talks.

41 See Council of the European Union, April 16, 2021, Conclusions on an EU Strategy the Indo-Pacific, https://data.consilium.europa.eu/doc/document/ST-7914-2021-INIT/en/pdf.

42 See The EU Strategy for Cooperation in the Indo-Pacific, European Commission, Joint Communication to the European Parliament and the Council September 16, 2021, https://eeas.europa.eu/sites/default/files/jointcommunication_2021_24_1_en.pdf

43 For details, see William A. Callahan., *China Dreams: 20 Visions for the Future*, Oxford University Press 2013.

Bibliography

Abi-Habib, Maria, *How China Got Sri Lanka to Cough up a Port*, New York Times, June 28, 2018, https://www.nytimes.com/2018/06/25/world/asia/china-sri-lanka-port.html

Bishton, Daniel, *Spratly Islands Military Bases Revealed*, Spatial Source, March 6, 2018, https://www.spatialsource.com.au/gis-data/satellite-images-reveal-completed-military-bases-spratly-islands

Buchan, Patrick Gerard and Rimland, Benjamin, *Defining the Diamond: The Past, Present, and Future of the Quadrilateral Security Dialogue*, CSIS Brief, Center for Strategic and International Studies (CSIS), March 16, 2020, https://www.csis.org/analysis/defining-diamond-past-present-and-future-quadrilateral-security-dialogue

Callahan, William A., *China Dreams: 20 Visions for the Future*, Oxford University Press, 2013.

Chaudhury, Rahul-Roy, *Understanding the UK's Tilt Towards the Indo-Pacific*, Chatham House Commentary, April 15, 2021, https://www.iiss.org/blogs/analysis/2021/04/uk-indo-pacific-tilt

Cheung, Rachel and Wilhelm, Benjamin, *Why China's 'Wolf-Warriors' Won't Back Down*, World Politics Review (WPR), April 7, 2021, https://www.worldpoliticsreview.com/trend-lines/29554/china-s-wolf-warrior-diplomacy-is-here-to-stay

China's Wolf-Warrior Gamble. Foreign Policy is not like an Action Film, The Economist, May 30, 2020.

Council of the European Union, April 16, 2021, Conclusions on an EU Strategy in the Indo-Pacific, https://data.consilium.europa.eu/doc/document/ST-7914-2021-INIT/en/pdf

Doyle, Timothy, *Blue Economy and the Ocean Rim*, Journal of the Indian Ocean Region, Vol. 14, 2018, pp. 1-6.

Duggal, Mahima, *The Case for a Britain-India-Japan Trilateral*, Council on Geostrategy, May 21,2021, https://www.geostrategy.org.uk/britains-world/the-case-for-a-britain-india-japan-trilateral/

Enhanced EU Security Cooperation in and with Asia, Council of the European Union, Brussels, May 28, 2018, https://www.consilium.europa.eu/media/35456/st09265-re01-en18.pdf

EU-China 2020 Strategic Agenda for Cooperation, European External Action Service (EEAS), 2020, https://eeas.europa.eu/archives/docs/china/docs/eu-china_2020_strategic_agenda_en.pdf

EU-China Investment Deal Leaves a Lot to be Desired, Merics China Briefing, January 14,

2021, https://merics.org/en/briefing/eu-china-investment-deal-leaves-lot-be-desired

France and Security in the Indo-Pacific, Ministère des Armes France, May 2019, https://www.defense.gouv.fr/layout/set/print/content/download/532754/9176250/version/3/file/France+and+Security+in+the+Indo-Pacific+-+2019.pdf

Fulda, Andreas, *Germany's New Policy Paper for the Indo-Pacific: Some Change in Tone, Little in Substance*, RUSI Commentary, September 11, 2020, https://rusi.org/commentary/germanys-new-policy-paper-indo-pacific-some-change-tone-little-substance

German-Europe-Asia. Shaping the 21st Century Together, Federal German Foreign Office, Berlin, August 2020, https://www.auswaertiges-amt.de/blob/2380514/f9784f7e3b3fa1bd7c5446d274a4169e/200901-indo-pazifik-leitlinien--1--data.pdf

Germany's Merkel Calls for Human Rights Dialogue with China, Reuters, April 28, 2021, https://www.reuters.com/world/china/merkel-calls-human-rights-dialogue-with-china-resume-2021-04-28/

Global Britain in a Competitive Age. The Integrated Review of Security, Defence, Development and Foreign Policy, March 2021, https://www.gov.uk/government/publications/global-britain-in-a-competitive-age-the-integrated-review-of-security-defence-development-and-foreign-policy

Griffith, James, *Beijing may have Built Bases in the South China Sea, but that doesn't mean it can Defend them, report claims*, CNN, December 7, 2020, https://edition.cnn.com/2020/12/07/china/south-china-sea-bases-military-intl-hnk/index.html

Hoang, Viet, *The Code of Conduct for the South China Sea: A Long and Bumpy Road*, The Diplomat, September 28, 2020; https://thediplomat.com/2020/09/the-code-of-conduct-for-the-south-china-sea-a-long-and-bumpy-road/

Huang, Kristin, *South China Sea: China has Extended another Spratly Islands Reef*, Photos Show, South China Morning Post, March 24, 2021, https://www.scmp.com/news/china/military/article/3126656/south-china-sea-beijing-has-extended-another-spratly-islands

In the South China Sea, America is Churning Waters Claimed by China, The Economist, July 25, 2020, https://www.economist.com/asia/2020/07/23/in-the-south-china-sea-america-is-churning-waters-claimed-by-china

Iyer, Gayathri, *Mega-ships in the Indian Ocean: Evaluating the Impact and Exploring Littoral Cooperation*, ORF Occasional Paper No. 204, Observer Research Foundation, July 2019, https://www.orfonline.org/research/mega-ships-in-the-indian-ocean-evaluating-the-impact-and-exploring-littoral-cooperation-53235/

Leithäuser, Johannes, *Deutschland Entsendet Fregatte in Ostasiatische Gewässer*, Frankfurter Allgemeine Zeitung, March 2, 2021, https://www.faz.net/aktuell/politik/inland/deutschland-entsendet-fregatte-in-indo-pazifik-raum-17224589.html

Mitchell, Tom and Mason, Katrina, Xi's Trade Deal with the EU Rings Alarm Bells in US, Financial Times, January 2, 2021

Mizorogi, Takuya, *Japan Woos Germany on Indo-Pacific with first 2-Plus-2 Talks*, Nikkei Asia, April 6, 2021, https://asia.nikkei.com/Politics/International-relations/Japan-woos-Germany-on-Indo-Pacific-with-first-2-plus-2-talks

Mohan, Garima, Germany Gets On Board With The Indo-Pacific, 9DashLine, September 11, 2020, https://www.9dashline.com/article/germany-gets-on-board-the-indo-pacific

Mohan, Garima, *A European Approach to the Indo-Pacific?*, Global Public Policy Institute, August 20, 2020, https://www.gppi.net/2020/08/20/a-european-approach-to-the-indo-pacific

Müller, Björn, *Marine Plant die Entsendung einer Fregatte in den Indo-Pazifik*, Pivot Area, November 26, 2019, https://www.pivotarea.eu/2019/11/26/fregatte-in-den-indo-pazifik/

Ramos, Cristia Marie, *UK, France, Germany Refute China's Expansive South China Sea Claims*, Inquirer.Net, September 18, 2020, https://globalnation.inquirer.net/190953/uk-france-germany-refute-chinas-expansive-south-china-sea-claims

Ryall, Julian, *Japan, Germany's First 2 Plus 2 Shows Extent of Tokyo's Outreach Amid China's Rising Assertiveness: Analysts*, South China Morning Post, April 5, 2021, https://www.scmp.com/week-asia/politics/article/3128366/japan-germanys-first-2-plus-2-dialogue-shows-extent-tokyos

Sharma, Kiran and Penne-Lassus, Mailys, *France to Lead Quad Naval Drill in Indo Pacific Challenge to China*, Nikkei Asia, April 2, 2021, https://asia.nikkei.com/Politics/International-relations/Indo-Pacific/France-to-lead-Quad-naval-drill-in-Indo-Pacific-challenge-to-China

Singh, Gurjit, *Germany Takes View of the Indo-Pacific*, Observer Research Foundation (ORF), October 1, 2020, https://www.orfonline.org/expert-speak/germany-takes-view-indo-pacific/

South China Sea: Satellite Images Show China Building Full-Blown Military Bases on Artificial Islands, NZHerald.co.nz, February 21, 2021; https://www.nzherald.co.nz/world/south-china-sea-satellite-images-show-china-building-full-blown-military-bases-on-artificial-islands/DAM22R4VYYCKYAZRPRION7ISXU/

The Quad is Finding its Purpose, at Last, The Economist, June 12, 2021, https://www.economist.com/asia/2021/06/12/the-quad-is-finding-its-purpose-at-last

The EU Strategy for Cooperation in the Indo-Pacific, European Commission, Joint Communication to the European Parliament and the Council September 16, 2021, https://eeas.europa.eu/sites/default/files/jointcommunication_2021_24_1_en.pdf

Tsuruoka, Michito and Kundnani, Hans, *Germany's Indo-Pacific Frigate May Send Unclear Message*, Chatham House Expert Comment, May 4, 2021, https://www.chathamhouse.org/2021/05/germanys-indo-pacific-frigate-may-send-unclear-message

Taiwan: Record Number of China Jets Enter Air Zone, BBC News, April 13, 2021, https://www.bbc.com/news/world-asia-56728072

EU-East Asia and EU-South Korea connectivity
From theory to practice

Ramon Pacheco Pardo

Introduction

Strengthening Eurasian connectivity has become a key goal for multiple actors across this landmass. ASEAN, China, India, Iran, Japan, Russia, South Korea, or Turkey have strategies to connect different parts of Eurasia—when not all of it. Physical, digital, and people-to-people are the three areas that these strategies emphasize, particularly the first two. Adopted in 2013, China's Belt and Road Initiative (BRI) is the best-known of these strategies. To an extent, most other initiatives are either a response to BRI or have evolved in recent years as a result of Beijing's initiative.

The EU is no stranger to this push to connect the different parts of Eurasia. Indeed, the Transport Corridor Europe-Caucasus-Asia (TRACECA) launched in 1993 was an early attempt to build the necessary infrastructure to connect Europe with Central Asia.[1] Meanwhile, the Asia-Europe Meeting (ASEM) established in 1996 was one of the pioneers in promoting people-to-people links between Europe and Asia[2], in particular through the Singapore based Asia Europe Foundation (ASEF).[3] It has only been in recent years and partially as a response to BRI, however, that the EU has taken physical and digital connectivity more seriously. The Connecting Europe & Asia strategy adopted in September

2018 was an is an attempt to promote connectivity on European terms. Its focus on physical infrastructure (formally divided into transport and energy), digital accessibility, and people-to-people links emphasizes the EU's holistic approach to connectivity.[4] This was reinforced in the Indo-Pacific strategy adopted in September 2021, which included connectivity as one of its seven key priorities—in a region that partly overlaps with Eurasia.[5]

Brussels, however, has been accused of focusing on talking rather than doing. Certainly, a crucial reason why BRI has become the dominant Eurasian connectivity platform is the amount of funding that the Chinese government, development banks, and state-owned enterprises are providing to the countries targeted by the initiative. Development agencies and firms from other countries with Eurasian strategies such as Japan or South Korea are also big providers of funding to different sub-regions, most notably Central Asia and South and Southeast Asia. The EU, however, has been unable to compete with these countries due to the lack of resources. The Global Gateway launched in November 2021 is Brussels' attempt to address this by mobilizing EU, member state, and private funding.[6]

In this chapter, I will first analyse the EU's Eurasia connectivity strategy with specific reference to East Asia. I will focus both on the EU's overall strategy and its bilateral component, with specific reference to Japan and India; then I will turn to the relevance for South Korea. I will focus on both, bilateral EU-South Korea cooperation, as well as potential for bilateral cooperation in East and South Asia. Finally, I will summarize the key points in the concluding section.

EU-East Asia connectivity

The 'Connecting Europe & Asia' strategy

In September 2018, the European Commission and the High Representative of the Union for Foreign Affairs and Security Policy (HRVP) issued the 'Connecting Europe and Asia – Building Blocks for an EU Strategy'. Three different developments led to this publication.

Firstly, Asia is the undisputed centre of economic growth, trade, and investment but with a hug need to develop the infrastructure of the continent. Due to the lack of a connectivity strategy with the exception of Central Asia the EU had become only a secondary actor. Secondly, Beijing's BRI had become the undisputed dominant connectivity strategy in the region. Even as other countries such as Japan and South Korea provided significant funding towards the region, the conversation was dominated by BRI. Although not officially admitted, the EU's strategy was an attempt to counter China's influence. Thirdly, the EU's concept promoted sustainable, comprehensive, and rules-based connectivity. In the view of policy-makers in Brussels, BRI did not apply any of these principles. Therefore, the EU could counter China's influence and expand its model by taking a values-driven approach to connectivity. Yet, the EU should consider that there are countries as critical of its emphasis on values as they are of China's allegedly harsh economic conditions.

In any case, the EU's strategy differs in its holistic approach to connectivity, from China's alleged narrow focus on physical infrastructure. Attending to the realities and needs of Asia, 'Connecting Europe and Asia' did emphasize physical connectivity, divided into transport and energy. In addition and stark contrast to China, the EU's strategy also focused on digital connectivity and the human dimension or people-to-people.[7] By taking this holistic approach, the EU could develop links at different levels, based on the needs and interests of the target countries and regions. Thereby it seeks to extend its influence across sectors.

The EU's emphasis on digital connectivity and people-to-people was in line with focus on areas in which it arguably has a comparative advantage. As for digital connectivity, there is no dominant actor at the global level and the rules of the game are yet to be set. In November 2018, only two months after 'Connecting Europe and Asia' strategy was published, the Commission issued its digital strategy.[8] Based on its yearlong experience the strategy showed the EU's ambition to create internationally acceptable standards. And the 'Connecting Europe and Asia' strategy even references the EU's Digital4Development strategy.[9]

Although, at the time of writing, the latter only focuses on Africa.[10] However, it could be expanded to include Asia in the future if there is a political consensus in the EU to do so.

With regard to people-to-people connectivity, the EU wants to play to its strengths as an education and research hub. Thus, 'Connecting Europe and Asia' emphasized that up to 18,000 students, researchers, and staff have benefited from EU mobility agreements.[11] Furthermore, Horizon 2020—replaced by Horizon Europe in 2021—promoted links between research and educational institutions in Europe and Asia to foster scientific innovation.[12] From the EU's perspective, Europe is an attractive partner and destination for students and researchers which explains the focus on this area.

While the EU is not a key player in the area of physical infrastructure in Asia, the Asian Development Bank (ADB), the World Bank, China, Japan, or South Korea are . The ADB forecasted in its 2017, 'developing Asia' report the need of US$26 trillion in infrastructure investment in the period 2016-30[13] a target impossible to meet. . Thus, there is ample space for other physical infrastructure providers in the region, a potential door opener for the EU., The European Investment Bank (EIB) already has projects in China, India, or Central Asia[14] while the EU-dominated European Bank for Reconstruction and Development (EBRD) run projects in Central Asia.[15] In sum, the EU has experience and continues to operate in these parts of Asia.

'Connecting Europe and Asia' follows a cooperative path at the bilateral, regional, and multilateral level.[16] The EU is aware that it can increase its influence through partnerships among equals. This would boost its lending capacity, since it would be able to combine its financial resources with those of its partners, and attend to the needs of the region. This reflects a welcome and necessary shift from the EU's earlier approaches to Asia, when Brussels gave the impression to suggest to Asian countries to follow Europe's economic development model.[17] This is exemplified by a specific reference to supporting the Master Plan on ASEAN Connectivity 2025[18] – instead of presenting itself as a model for ASEAN, the EU sought to partner with ASEAN to contribute to

ASEAN's connectivity strategy.

Nevertheless, For two main reasons 'Connecting Europe and Asia' failed to upraise the position of the EU as a connectivity actor in Asia: Firstly, the EU was not able to mobilize the financing vehicles earmarked to strengthen its presence in the region: the Investment Facility for Central Asia, the Asian Investment Facility, and the European Fund for Sustainable Development were not mobilized to the extent necessary to make a difference. The funding provided by the EIB or EBRD was certainly useful for the recipient countries but not deal-breakers. Money talks but in relation to Asian connectivity, the EU simply did not have the funds to make it talk. Secondly, 'Connecting Europe and Asia' came at a time when the conversation had already moved towards the concept of the Indo-Pacific. Indo-Pacific strategies covered not only a larger geographical scope, but also recognised the geostrategic competition between the US and its partners and China . This is not to say that BRI or other connectivity strategies did not have a geopolitical component. They certainly did. But Washington's push of the Indo-Pacific concept under President Donald Trump put geopolitics front and centre. Connectivity, therefore, became one of several areas part of this competition.

The Indo-Pacific strategy

In September 2021, the Commission and the HRVP issued 'The EU Strategy for Cooperation in the Indo-Pacific'. To its credit, the EU moved swiftly by its own standards to come up with a credible Indo-Pacific strategy. Similarly to 'Connecting Europe and Asia', the Indo-Pacific strategy emphasizes the EU's greater engagement with the region, working with partners, and values in the form of a 'rules-based international order'.[19] The Indo-Pacific strategy shows that the EU is aware of the need to become an active player in the most dynamic world region from an economic, political, and security perspective; the need to work with partners to enhance the EU's role within the region; and the potential benefits of emphasizing values as an entry point to develop a distinct regional presence. While the Indo-Pacific strategy was a response to similar strategies by the US, Australia, India, Japan, or South Korea, all 'like-minded' partners, it was also response bo Beijing which does not fall into this category.

The EU's Indo-Pacific strategy covers seven priority areas: sustainable and inclusive prosperity, green transition, ocean governance, digital governance and partnerships, *connectivity* (emphasis added), security and defence, and human security.[20] Thus, Brussels placed connectivity at the core of its Indo-Pacific strategy while linking it to other areas that are central to the economic growth and prosperity of the region. Comparing the Indo-Pacific and 'Connecting Europe and Asia' the connectivity concept was included in some of the seven priorities listed in the Indo-Pacific strategy as connectivity is a cross-cutting issue and may be understood in different ways.

The EU's Indo-Pacific strategy confirmed that the EU's connectivity strategy is based on three principles: sustainability, comprehensiveness, and rules-based. The strategy is addressed to the EU institutions, member states, and the private sector. This 'Team Europe' in EU speak is necessary to develop connectivity projects. Digital and transport connectivity are the two areas the EU wants to focus on in the Indo-Pacific region and, inclusion, in Asia. Digital connectivity covers both the digitalization of the region and the promotion of Brussels' regulatory and policy environment. Within transport connectivity the EU focus is on air transport agreements, dialogues, and infrastructure in a cooperative manner with partners and regional institutions.[21]

The cross-cutting nature of connectivity is also demonstrated by dealing with Transport connectivity as part of sustainable and inclusive prosperity and green transition of the Indo Pacific strategy.[22] Energy is dealt with as part of green transition.[23] Digital connectivity has its own section, labelled digital governance and partnerships with a strong focus on digitalization and the promotion of European standards.[24] The people-to-people dimension was included in the digital connectivity component of the EU's strategy under research and innovation, as well as education.[25]

Considering that like-minded partners with strong economic capabilities such as Australia, Japan, South Korea, or the US have their own approaches to the Indo-Pacific, there is scope for the EU to implement the connectivity component of its strategy in cooperation with partners. In particular, the Biden administration has realized that a big flaw of Trump's Indo-Pacific strategy was the absence of any infrastructure-development component. The Indo-Pacific Economic Framework is an attempt by the Biden administration to address this shortcoming.[26] If the EU wants to seriously influence connectivity in the Indo-Pacific region, joint work together with Washington's and other strategies would be the most promising approach.

The Global Gateway

In December 2021, the Commission and the HRVP issued 'The Global Gateway'. This is an attempt to address the main criticism of the previous EU connectivity strategy the lack of funding. The Global Gateway focuses squarely on infrastructure development, with a focus on physical infrastructure in the areas of digital, energy, and transport. It spells out a concrete figure, up to €300 billion in the period 2021-27 , implemented by Team Europe.[27] The Global Gateway was launched by the Ursula von der Leyen Commission, which characterised itself as a 'Geopolitical Commission'.[28] The EU wants to move beyond being an economic powerhouse to become a geopolitical power mobilizing its economic musclesto achieve its goals.

Like the Indo-Pacific strategy Global Gateway emphasizes cooperation with like-minded partners, including the US, Canada, India, Japan, and South Korea—as well as with ASEAN.[29] Even though it is a global strategy as the name indicates, there is no doubt that Asia is a key target region. Most notably, Global Gateway builds on 'Connecting Europe and Asia' among other documents.[30] Therefore, if the EU is able to mobilize the necessary capital, billions of euros will be spent in Asia when bringing together public and private capital. Thus, the EU would finally be recognized as an actor in the connectivity of the continent.

The EU's connectivity agreements with Japan and India

The EU constantly underscores the importance of working with partners to develop its connectivity pledge. This is not only rhetoric. It is a necessity, particularly when the EU wants to be a connectivity actor in Asia. To this end, the EU and Japan signed a connectivity strategy in September 2019. The EU and India followed suit in May 2021. The two of them are referenced in the EU's Indo-Pacific strategy and Global Gateway. The EU would also confirms its interest to sign connectivity strategies with ASEAN and South Korea.

The connectivity agreement by Brussels and Tokyo was labelled 'The Partnership on Sustainable Connectivity and Quality Infrastructure between the European Union and Japan'.[31] The name is very telling. The implicit assumption is that other connectivity projects are neither sustainable nor high-quality. In other words, the EU and Japan want to counter China with their superior model. The strategy focuses on digital, transport, energy, and people-to-people connectivity in third countries in cooperation with other projects. Brussels and Tokyo deem it necessary to develop an international consortium to counter the influence of BRI.

The agreement signed by Brussels and Delhi, meanwhile, is labelled 'EU-India Connectivity Partnership'.[32] The strategy focuses on digital, transport, energy, and people-to-people as well. It focuses both on strengthening connectivity between the EU and India and also with third countries. t India is recognised as a key country to build connectivity links, also with other developing countries in other regions.

These bilateral agreements signed by the EU highlight the potential for Brussels to develop a network of links within Asia to implement its connectivity strategy. The shortcoming is that the EU and Japan and India respectively have not been able to develop any joint project (at the time of writing). This can potentially undermine the EU's emphasis on working with partners and may even deter others to join the EU. Japan, has a decades-old experience in developing infrastructure projects in Southeast Asia. Its government, development agencies, and private firms may see no incentive to cooperate with Europe in this area. India, is a target country of the connectivity strategies of China, Japan, and South

Korea. It also has a long-standing relations with the ADB. Therefore, Delhi may not see any utility to adhere to the conditionality of more stringent EU standards in exchange for access to EU funding if other sources are available.

EU-Korea connectivity cooperation in Asia

The EU has a clear connectivity strategy for Asia. It encompasses physical infrastructure plus digital infrastructure, as well as people-to-people. The first two elements—physical and digital—are prioritized by Brussels as it has become more geopolitical and attentive to the priorities of the region. The EU's connectivity strategy is built on cooperation with like-minded partners to amplify its strengths as an infrastructure provider. At least in theory values are a cornerstone of the strategy. pursuing a sustainable, comprehensive, and rules-based connectivity.

South Korea is a natural partner for the EU. South Korea is the only Asian partner with the three key agreements covering politics, economics, and security in place as of 2021. This means, the EU considers South Korea to be among its strongest partners in the region. Only Japan can match the strength of the bonds that Brussels and Seoul have forged over the past decade. This strong and sustainable framework has created the basis for deep bilateral ties as well as for cooperation at the international level.

At the time of writing the EU and South Korea have digital and energy dialogues, and are discussing the launch of a transport dialogue as well. These dialogues would cover the three key areas of the EU's Asia connectivity strategy. The EU has identified South Korea as its preferred connectivity partners in all three recent policy papers, 'Connecting Europe and Asia', Indo-Pacific strategy, and the Global Gateway. South Korea is also cited as a like-minded partner in the last of these two documents. Therefore, Brussels and Seoul have a framework in place to develop a robust connectivity cooperation in Asia.

Within Asia, South Asia—especially India—and Southeast Asia are the two sub-regions prone for cooperation between the EU and South Korea te. The EU's reference to South Korea's Indo-Pacific strategy is an implicit reference to its New Southern Policy Plus strategy. This policy aims at boosting ties with Southeast Asia and India, including physical and digital infrastructure.[33] Thereby Seoul has found the means to strengthen links with Southeast Asia and India it was looking for for many years. With the New Southern Policy Plus, the Moon Jae-in government established a clear framework that future presidents are likely to build on even if the name of their strategy may change.

What are the potential areas of practical connectivity cooperation between the EU and South Korea? In the area of physical connectivity, airports, railroads, roads, and other infrastructure projects that countries in South and Southeast Asia currently lack. Brussels and Seoul can also focus on supply chain resilience, which has become important as a result of the COVID-19 pandemic. The EU and South Korea can also strive with other partners such as Japan or the US to mobilize more capital and expertise. In pursuing their preference for sustainable and high-quality infrastructure, the EU and Korea should be able to find at least one joint project.[34]

In the area of digital connectivity, the EU and South Korea can focus on the development of physical infrastructure (e.g., fibre-optic cables or 5G), the development of universal standards and norms, and the resilience of digital networks. This would include a combination of specific projects with countries in South and Southeast Asia seeking to upgrade their infrastructure, as well as working within multilateral institutions and regimes to promote globally agreed standards. Similarly to the case of digital infrastructure, it should be possible to find at least one project for.[35]

There is a question as to whether the EU and South Korea should sign a connectivity partnership agreement, comparable to those already signed by the EU with Japan and India. Such an agreement would symbolize the commitment of the two partners to collaborate in this area. It would also provide the written framework to develop cooperation activities. Through such a partnership potential partners in South and Southeast Asia would be made aware of the commitment to cooperate in the region by Brussels and Seoul. While such an agreement would not be legally binding, its non-implementation would put into doubt the commitment of both partners to cooperate. Since the EU has not launched any project with Japan more than two years after the two had signed their agreement, these are points to consider. This problem could be solved if Brussels and Seoul only sign a partnership when they launch a concrete cooperation project.

Conclusion

The EU has a well-developed Asia connectivity strategy. The principles are clear, cooperation with partners is essential. Implementing the connectivity strategy will allow the EU to become a more active player in the region, strengthen like-minded partners, and counter the influence of BRI. This is an excellent starting point to gain influence through the promotion connectivity in East Asia, the sub-region that the EU is prioritizing. The EU is not a relevant player in the sub-region at the time of writing. But it has the potential to become one, particularly if it becomes a geopolitical actor.

This will only happen if the EU moves from theory to practice. Brussels has been criticized for not devoting the necessary financial resources to follow through on its strategies. The Global Gateway has the potential to address this criticism by providing the EU with the necessary financial muscle to implement its connectivity strategy, including towards East Asia. The idea of forging a Team Europe bringing together EU institutions and its member states, as well as working on mobilizing the private sector could serve to finally enable the EU to develop a wide range of large-scale infrastructure projects.

South Korea should work together with the EU to develop connectivity projects, with South and Southeast Asia as the priorities but potentially in other regions as well. Brussels and Seoul are like-minded partners, they have a cooperation framework in place, and both of them have the necessary financial capabilities and expertise to boost cooperation in this area. The EU is indeed calling for cooperation with South Korea in the area of connectivity. Seoul should heed Brussels' call. This would benefit both partners, and would fit within South Korea's long-standing goal to become a recognized global actor.

---

1 Transport Corridor Europe-Caucasus-Asia, *TRACECA*, 2021, available at http://www.traceca-org.org/en/home/ (accessed 15 December 2021).

2 ASEM InfoBoard, *Asia-Europe Meeting*, 2021, available at https://www.aseminfoboard.org/ (accessed 15 December 2021).

3 Asia-Europe Foundation, *Asia-Europe Foundation*, 2022, available at https://asef.org/ (accessed 21 February 2022).

4 European Commission and High Representative of the Union for Foreign Affairs and Security Policy, *Connecting Europe and Asia – Building Blocks for an EU Strategy*, Brussels, 19 September 2018.

5 European Commission and High Representative of the Union for Foreign Affairs and Security Policy, *The EU Strategy for Cooperation in the Indo-Pacific*, Brussels, 16 September 2021.

6 European Commission and High Representative of the Union for Foreign Affairs and Security Policy, *The Global Gateway*, Brussels, 1 December 2021.

7 European Commission and High Representative of the Union for Foreign Affairs and Security Policy, *Connecting Europe and Asia – Building Blocks for an EU Strategy*, pp. 3-6.

8 European Commission, *European Commission Digital Strategy – A Digitally Transformed, User-focused and Data-Driven Commission*, Brussels, 21 November 2018.

9 European Commission and High Representative of the Union for Foreign Affairs and Security Policy, *Connecting Europe and Asia – Building Blocks for an EU Strategy*, p. 5.

10 EU D4D Coalition, *D4D Hub*, 2021, available at https://d4dlaunch.eu/#about (accessed 15 December 2021).

11 European Commission and High Representative of the Union for Foreign Affairs and Security Policy, *Connecting Europe and Asia – Building Blocks for an EU Strategy*, p. 6.

12 European Commission, *Horizon Europe*, 2021, available at https://ec.europa.eu/info/research-and-innovation/funding/funding-opportunities/funding-programmes-and-open-calls/horizon-europe_en (accessed 15 December 2021).

13 Asian Development Bank, *Meeting Asia's Infrastructure Needs* (Manila: Asian Development Bank, 2017), p. vii.

14 European Investment Bank, The EIB in Asia and Latin America, 2021, available at https://www.eib.org/en/projects/regions/ala/index.htm (accessed 15 December 2021); European Investment Bank, *The EIB in Central Asia*, 2021, available at https://www.eib.org/en/projects/regions/central-asia/index.htm (accessed 15 December 2021).

15 European Bank for Reconstruction and Development, *Where We Are*, 2021, available at https://www.ebrd.com/where-we-are.html (accessed 15 December 2021).

16 European Commission and High Representative of the Union for Foreign Affairs and Security Policy, *Connecting Europe and Asia – Building Blocks for an EU Strategy*, pp. 7-9.

17 See, for example, Commission of the European Communities, *Towards a New Asia Strategy*, 13 July 1994.

18 European Commission and High Representative of the Union for Foreign Affairs and Security Policy, *Connecting Europe and Asia – Building Blocks for an EU Strategy*, p. 8.

19 European Commission and High Representative of the Union for Foreign Affairs and Security Policy, *The EU Strategy for Cooperation in the Indo-Pacific*,.

20 European Commission and High Representative of the Union for Foreign Affairs and Security Policy, *The EU Strategy for Cooperation in the Indo-Pacific*, p. 5.

21 Ibid., pp. 12-13

22 Ibid., pp. 6, 8, 9.

23 Ibid., pp 8-9.

24 Ibid., pp. 10-11.

25 Ibid., p. 11.

26 The White House, *Readout of President Biden's Participation in the East Asia Summit*, Washington, DC, 27 October 2021.

27 European Commission and High Representative of the Union for Foreign Affairs and Security Policy, *The Global Gateway*, Brussels, 1 December 2021, pp. 1-2.

28 European Commission, 'Speech by President-elect von der Leyen in the European Parliament Plenary on the Occasion of the Presentation of her College of Commissioners and their Programme', Strasbourg, 27 November 2019.

29 European Commission and High Representative of the Union for Foreign Affairs and Security Policy, *The Global Gateway*, p. 12.

30 Ibid., p. 2.

31 European External Action Service, *The Partnership on Sustainable Connectivity and Quality Infrastructure between the European Union and Japan*, Brussels, 27 September 2019.

32 European Council, *EU-India Connectivity Partnership*, 8 May 2021.

33 New Southern Policy, *New Southern Policy*, 2021, available at http://www.nsp.go.kr/eng/main.do (accessed 15 December 2021).

34 Desmaele, Linde, Maximilian Ernst, Tongfi Kim, Ramon Pacheco Pardo and Michael Reiterer, *The EU's Indo-Pacific Strategy: Prospects for Cooperation with South Korea* (Brussels: KF-VUBV Korea Chair, 2021), pp. 17-24.

35 Ibid., pp. 24-31.

Bibliography

ASEM InfoBoard, *Asia-Europe Meeting*, 2021, available at https://www.aseminfoboard.org/ (accessed 15 December 2021)

Asian Development Bank, *Meeting Asia's Infrastructure Needs* (Manila: Asian Development Bank, 2017)

Asia-Europe Foundation, *Asia-Europe Foundation*, 2022, available at https://asef.org/ (accessed 21 February 2022).

Commission of the European Communities, *Towards a New Asia Strategy*, 13 July 1994.

Desmaele, Linde, Maximilian Ernst, Tongfi Kim, Ramon Pacheco Pardo and Michael Reiterer, *The EU's Indo-Pacific Strategy: Prospects for Cooperation with South Korea* (Brussels: KF-VUBV Korea Chair, 2021)

EU D4D Coalition, *D4D Hub*, 2021, available at https://d4dlaunch.eu/#about (accessed 15 December 2021).

European Bank for Reconstruction and Development, *Where We Are*, 2021, available at https://www.ebrd.com/where-we-are.html (accessed 15 December 2021).

European Commission, *European Commission Digital Strategy – A Digitally Transformed, User-focused and Data-Driven Commission*, Brussels, 21 November 2018.

European Commission, *Horizon Europe*, 2021, available at https://ec.europa.eu/info/research-and-innovation/funding/funding-opportunities/funding-programmes-and-open-calls/horizon-europe_en (accessed 15 December 2021).

European Commission, 'Speech by President-elect von der Leyen in the European Parliament Plenary on the Occasion of the Presentation of her College of Commissioners and their Programme', Strasbourg, 27 November 2019.

European Commission and High Representative of the Union for Foreign Affairs and Security Policy, *Connecting Europe and Asia – Building Blocks for an EU Strategy*, Brussels, 19 September 2018.

European Commission and High Representative of the Union for Foreign Affairs and Security Policy, *The Global Gateway*, Brussels, 1 December 2021.

European Commission and High Representative of the Union for Foreign Affairs and Security Policy, *The EU Strategy for Cooperation in the Indo-Pacific*, Brussels, 16 September 2021.

European Council, *EU-India Connectivity Partnership*, 8 May 2021.

European External Action Service, *The Partnership on Sustainable Connectivity and Quality Infrastructure between the European Union and Japan*, Brussels, 27 September 2019.

European Investment Bank, *The EIB in Asia and Latin America*, 2021, available at https://

www.eib.org/en/projects/regions/ala/index.htm (accessed 15 December 2021)

European Investment Bank, *The EIB in Central Asia*, 2021, available at https://www.eib.org/en/projects/regions/central-asia/index.htm (accessed 15 December 2021).

New Southern Policy, *New Southern Policy*, 2021, available at http://www.nsp.go.kr/eng/main.do (accessed 15 December 2021).

The White House, *Readout of President Biden's Participation in the East Asia Summit*, Washington, DC, 27 October 2021.

Transport Corridor Europe-Caucasus-Asia, *TRACECA*, 2021, available at http://www.traceca-org.org/en/home/ (accessed 15 December 2021).

Connecting Europe and South Korea within the US-China Conflict

Tereza Novotná

Introduction

The chapter examines the ways in which the EU and South Korea can cope with the conflict between the US and China both as the result of a shorter-term COVID-19 crisis and of previous underlying long-term trends. The chapter suggests that the EU should intensify cooperation with the Republic of Korea (ROK) as the key country in North East Asia which is in a similar situation of "being caught between the US and China". The chapter argues that the EU and ROK should: firstly, strengthen their Strategic Partnership, especially in the areas of common interest such as health, digital connectivity and climate change; secondly, identify areas where the EU and ROK can pre-empt the Sino-American rivalry from escalating by coming up with joint proposals that would be acceptable both to the US and China (e.g. North Korea); and, thirdly, create a network of like-minded partners in South/South East Asia (e.g. ASEAN countries) and Indo-Pacific (e.g. New Zealand, possibly Canada) to offset any tensions between the US and China.

> "...perhaps the best way is to see COVID-19 as the great accelerator of history. It strengthens trends that were already present before... everywhere we look we see increasing rivalries, especially between the US and China. The pressure to choose sides is growing. As EU, we should follow our own

> interests and values and avoid being instrumentalised by one or the other. We need a more robust strategy for China, which also requires better relations with the rest of democratic Asia. That's why we must invest more in working with India, Japan, South Korea et cetera."
>
> Josep Borrell, 25 May 2020

This section of the speech[1] held at the German Ambassadors' conference by the High Representative of the Union for Foreign Affairs (HRVP) Josep Borrell nearly two years ago in May 2020 is still valid. Borrell outlined the long-term geopolitical challenges for the European Union (EU) which were reinforced by the COVID-19 crisis. He follows on his predecessor, HRVP Federica Mogherini, who included a chapter on a "Connected Asia" into her signature 2016 EU Global Strategy.[2] While the Global Strategy coined the term "EU's strategic autonomy", the section on Asia emphasizes expansion of the EU's partnerships across Asia, including with South Korea.

This chapter examines the ways in which the EU and ROK can cope with the world emerging after the pandemic in the light of the conflict between the US and China. It views the Sino-American rivalry both as the short-term result of the COVID-19 crisis and a consequence of previous underlying long-term trends. Since both the EU and ROK face a similar challenge of "being caught between the US and China", and because ROK (next to Japan) is the key counterpart for the EU in North East (NE) Asia, the chapter suggests that Brussels and Seoul should prioritize strengthening of their Strategic Partnership which celebrated its 12th anniversary in October 2022. Solidifying the past results of the partnership towards a future cooperation will connect Europe and South Korea for their mutual benefit.

The chapter therefore argues that the EU and ROK should: firstly, intensify their joint cooperation, especially in the areas "connecting" their common interests such as health, digitalization and climate change. Secondly, the two partners should identify areas where they can pre-empt the Sino-American rivalry from escalating by developing common proposals that would be acceptable to both the US and

China. In this regard, a combined engagement on North Korea would be a good starting point. Thirdly, Brussels and Seoul should create a network of like-minded partners in South/South East Asia (e.g. ASEAN countries) and Indo-Pacific (e.g. New Zealand, potentially Canada) that also face the unenviable situation of having to choose sides between the two superpowers.

After introductory remarks, the chapter first outlines the broader geopolitical context of the US-China tensions from Presidents Trump to Biden and places the EU and ROK within it. The chapter proceeds with mapping several areas that are most suitable for an intensified collaboration between Brussels and Seoul. North Korea is an example where even though the US-China disagreements have so far been muted, the two superpowers are increasingly more likely to face off one another. The chapter concludes with suggesting that like-minded partners might want to join and create a network of states that do not want to choose either the US, or China, but may want to collaborate more closely with the EU and the ROK instead.

From Trump to Biden
Connecting Europe and South Korea within the US-China Conflict

The European view on how the Trump Administration has approached China – including its role at the start of the COVID-19 pandemic – has been ambivalent at best. On the one hand, Brussels shared Washington's concerns about the unknown origins of the SARS-CoV-2 and the handling of the illness by Beijing, such as the lack of transparency by the Chinese authorities. Even though the Europeans may have disliked President Trump's rhetoric about the "China virus", Beijing did not endear itself to them by a rather clumsy "mask diplomacy" towards various EU Member States, its aggressive statements and, domestically, by repressive measures against any critics condemning the Chinese intransigent approach.

On the other hand, the delayed and ineffectual response to the dangers of COVID-19 by the Trump Administration has made the US a dubious leader and ally in the eyes of many Europeans in the fight against the common enemy – SARS-CoV-2. Moreover, these developments were accompanied by Trump's "withdrawal doctrine".[3] President Trump left the World Health Organization (WHO) in the midst of a health emergency. He also pulled the rug under the Iran nuclear deal, the Paris Climate Accord, UNESCO, INF Treaty and others. By doing so, he shook the pillars of the multilateral world order. Therefore, the EU leaders stepped in to salvage these institutions throughout the Trump's years. They drummed up support among other partners interested in rescuing multilateral institutions, including Seoul.

The Europeans were happy to see Joe Biden, a life-long friend of the Old Continent to step into the Oval Office and to declare shortly after his inauguration that "America is back".[4] President Biden indeed reversed many of the actions of his predecessor. Within the first days and weeks of his presidency, the US re-joined the Paris climate agreement, WHO and others, returned to the negotiating table with Iran and slashed tariffs imposed on Europe in the past.

In the policy towards China, there has however been much more continuity between Biden and Trump than between Biden and Obama and his other democratic predecessors. Although Trump's presidency has been clearly marked by a harsh anti-Chinese rhetoric, the Biden-Harris team's China policy has so far been based on hard – or one would be tempted to say "smart" – power. However, in contrast to Trump's "America First" policy, and perhaps more in tune with the pre-Obama Democratic Presidents, the Biden Administration has been adamant on mobilizing support for its containment of China among its allies in Europe and Asia.

The so-called AUKUS deal and the Quad illustrate Biden's renewed emphasis on recruiting allies to face up to China. While AUKUS put Europe in a tough spot, Quad does the same to South Korea. Under the AUKUS security pact,[5] Australia will build nuclear-powered submarines with technology provided by the US (which has been previously shared only with the UK). This will enable Australia to better prepare itself to counter any aggressive moves by China in the Indo-Pacific. While the AUKUS pact has naturally been denounced by the Chinese authorities as "damaging regional peace... and intensifying the arms race,"[6] it has simultaneously created a rift with the Europeans. By teaming up with the US and UK, Australia withdrew from a multibillion-dollar deal with France to provide 12 traditional submarines.

The French (who were supported by most of the Europeans, including President of the European Council Charles Michel[7]), were not only appalled by losing a commercial deal, but also by the fact that AUKUS has been agreed behind France's back. Although Presidents Macron and Biden have since then mended their relationship, France clearly no longer sees Australia as a reliable and transparent ally: Paris dropped Canberra from its list of key partners in the Indo-Pacific[8] and vowed to cooperate only on a case-by-case basis. It is nonetheless the US policy to push back on China that had motivated Australia to rescind its agreement with France and to opt for more lethal (and more expensive) defensive capabilities.

Bolstering the Quad – a quadruple alliance between the US, Japan, Australia and India – is another feature of Biden's reliance on hard power vis-à-vis China. The Quad aims at strengthening the US position in the Indo-Pacific while limiting any space for Chinese economic and political expansion. While AUKUS has been a difficult pill to swallow for the French (and the Europeans), South Korea has been in a similar bind regarding the Quad. For South Korea, any participation in a Quad+ arrangement is tricky, firstly because of its apprehension of alienating China and secondly because of the prominent position of Japan within the Quad. For historical reasons, Japan has been Korea's and particularly its progressive governments' historical archnemesis.

Seoul could only join the Quad as a nucleus of "Asia's NATO", if – in paraphrasing Lord Ismay's famous saying about the purpose of NATO as an alliance to "keep the Soviet Union out, the Americans in, and the Germans down"[9]- it meets three conditions: to keep North Korea in as one of the key agenda points, to keep China out as its main rationale and to keep Japan's influence down as much as possible. Korea's triple wish is nonetheless not very likely to happen partly because China has undoubtedly been the Quad's key target, but also because the Quad's statements tend to highlight Tokyo's priorities vis-à-vis the DPRK, i.e., referring to "denuclearization of North Korea" (rather than the Korean peninsula) as well as solving the abductee issue.

Like Donald Trump who had a better rapport with his Japanese rather than South Korean counterparts, Joe Biden may have the same preferences, much to the chagrin of Seoul. This despite the fact that for a bit more than a year, both the White and Blue Houses have been occupied by progressive presidents. Whether these personal relationships will change and Seoul joins (officially or unofficially) the Quad once the new conservative South Korean President Yoon Suk-yeol takes the office, remains to be seen.

All in all, although Biden has followed in Trump's footsteps on China, his preference on utilizing the alliances – albeit selectively – to pursue the American interests may prove to be a bigger challenge for leaders in Europe and Asia than Trump's outright heavy-handed intimidation: standing up to coercion is easier than refusing a request by a close friend.

From Chinese "Wolf Warrior" Diplomats to Sanctions

Connecting Europe and South Korea within the US-China Conflict

It is, however, not only the EU relationship with the US which has become more antagonistic since the Trump Presidency. The Chinese Communist Party leaders have clearly become more assertive and do not shy away from using belligerent language particularly on social media, including trolls, propaganda and statements by "wolf warrior" diplomats posted to European capitals. Moreover, China uses violence to deliver the same message of strength: Beijing's attempts to suppress the protests against the extradition and national security laws in Hong Kong, and harsh words against anyone who stands up for the Hong Kongers, including the UK and other governments, are cases in point.

In addition, Beijing has also been willing to employ other ruthless tactics against foreign countries and nationals, including "hostage diplomacy" (e.g. the cases of two Canadians[10] who were arbitrarily detained in China for nearly three years in retaliation for the arrest of Huawei's CFO Meng Wanzhou on the behest of the US), an old-fashioned espionage (e.g. the case of a former EU Ambassador to Korea[11] who has allegedly been spying for China) and weaponization of trade (e.g. trade tariffs against Australia after Prime Minister Morrison had been vocal in calling for investigating the genesis of COVID-19 and China's responsibility for it).

Worries that a similar tool of coercion could be aimed at EU citizens and countries as a retribution for political actions that go against China's wishes emerged after the speaker of the Czech Senate visited Taiwan with a large business delegation in the late August 2020. Although China's Foreign Minister Wang Yi warned that the Senate speaker would "pay a heavy price"[12] for "crossing the line" of One China policy, this incident eventually resulted only in mutual summons of ambassadors in Prague and Beijing and in retraction of an order of several pianos[13] produced by a Czech family firm. Moreover, Czechia received a solid backing from other European governments, including Germany and France, whose foreign ministers expressed their strong displeasure over Beijing's reaction.

In another instance, Lithuania has experienced a more consequential retaliation by the Chinese authorities than Czechia after it had allowed to open a "Taiwanese Representative Office", rather than "Taipei's", in Vilnius. Since then, Lithuania has to put up with an embargo on all its exports to China.[14] China also threatened other European businesses with secondary restrictions on their products containing any Lithuania-made components. Although Vilnius received a similar backing as Prague, it came from the European Commission rather than from other member states.

In the end, the WTO will decide on the merits of the Chinese import controls. In January 2022, the European Commission brought a case before the WTO against China,[15] accusing it using discriminatory and illegal practices against Lithuania. Although the economic pressure by China continues at the time of writing, the European Commission protects not only a small member state, but also the European Single Market which has been adversely affected by Chinese coercion. The case of Lithuania – and the strength with which the EU has countered China's actions – may contribute to generating a more unified European stance on China (and Taiwan) in the future.

Quandaries getting out of hand and catching world-wide attention are not limited to politicians: A member of Korea's most popular K-pop boy band, BTS, enraged Chinese netizens after receiving an award for promoting US-Korea relations.[16] In his acceptance speech, the singer "RM" referred to 2020 as an especially meaningful year for the award because of the 70th anniversary of the Korean War. He remembered those Americans and South Koreans who sacrificed their lives, but "forgot" to mention the thousands of killed Chinese who had nonetheless fought on the other – North Korean – side in the "War to Resist the US Aggression and Aid Korea".[17] RM angered his Chinese fanbase and prompted Samsung, Fila and other companies to remove BTS merchandise from Chinese online platforms. A senior official from Beijing's ministry of foreign affairs had to intervene to calm the situation.[18]

These three episodes illustrate how difficult it might be for European and South Korean governments and individuals to position themselves between China and the US. Even though some of the animosities between Washington and Beijing might be smoothed out thanks to skilled diplomats hired to work for the Biden team, there is the danger that the current hostility between the two big powers turns into a long-term systemic competition between autocracies and democracies and a new version of Cold War.

Given the bipartisan consensus over the threat of a rising China among US policy-makers, the Sino-American rivalry may remain the defining feature for the years and US administrations to come. This leaves the EU – as well as other "middle powers" such as ROK – in an unappealing predicament of having to chart a course between the two superpowers, China and the US. As the saying about a "shrimp among whales"[19] goes, it no longer refers only to (South) Korea, but the EU is increasingly squeezed between China and the US in a very similar way.

Connecting Europe and South Korea Through Strengthening Their Strategic Partnership

Given Europe's and South Korea's position between the two superpowers, one could ask: What can the two like-minded partners do to avoid being pushed to one side or the other? To alleviate the pressure, the EU and ROK could strengthen their strategic partnership in putting emphasis on areas that have so far been less central to the relationship but are becoming increasingly relevant, such as health, digital connectivity and climate.

From the South Korean perspective, there is an additional bonus: North Korea can be included into all these areas. This might not only help restarting negotiations with the DPRK, but also contribute to preventing Pyongyang from leaning too much towards the Chinese side and/or becoming another theater of tensions between Washington and Beijing.

Connecting the European and South Korean Fights Against COVID-19

On the COVID-19 front, South Korea and China represent two poles on a continuum on how public institutions can cope with the pandemic. On one side of the spectrum, Beijing has since early on focused on a "zero Covid strategy" using "mass lockdowns" and other harsh measures as the key instrument to combat the spread of SARS-CoV-2. On the other hand, Seoul focused on "mass testing", creativity and transparency via its "test, trace and treat"[20] programme. EU member states have been fluctuating between these two approaches – with, for instance, Madrid and Paris opting more often for the Chinese-style strict lockdowns, while Berlin and Helsinki going in the South Korean direction with ubiquitous testing.

The European Commission has been impressed by South Korea's pandemic management and, as a token of appreciation for Seoul's success, South Korean citizens have always been allowed to enter the EU[21] without obligation to self-isolate upon arrival. Although the Korean authorities were criticized by the Europeans for having to quarantine upon entering South Korea, Chinese nationals would have been accorded the same privilege of free EU admission had there been reciprocity by Beijing – which has never materialized given entry and quarantine "zero Covid" measures on the Chinese side. Brussels was also pleased when Seoul pledged over 45 million euro to the European Commission's COVID-19 Global Response fund,[22] thus matching China's contribution. Similarly, the "Team Europe"[23] has been delighted when ROK committed to join Gavi's COVAX facility[24] which supports equitable access to SARS-CoV-2 vaccine. In addition to the personal protective equipment (PPE) production and supply chains, Brussels and Seoul have proved to be fitting partners in fighting COVID-19 both in terms of shared teamwork and solidarity with third parties.

Once COVID-vaccines became available and the second phase of the pandemic started, South Korea began lagging behind Europe[25] in terms of their procurement. Nonetheless, the South Koreans have quickly caught up and reached higher inoculation rates than in Europe due to their lower vaccine hesitancy. Seoul has also vowed to become a vaccine production hub in Asia – mostly through franchising with pharma companies and producing "K-vaccines" based on the European know-how. Yet the Omicron wave has thrown spanner in the works and Europe as well as South Korea have seen spiking numbers of SARS-CoV-2 cases. Nonetheless, as horrendous as it is, the pandemic has brought Brussels and Seoul closer together in a previously under-explored health sector, while simultaneously helping the EU and ROK maintain a healthy distance from the US and China.

In terms of North Korea, the pandemic could also help enhance engagement with Pyongyang at the humanitarian level. Contrary to various speculations, an early shutdown of the DPRK borders[26], a possible early warning by Chinese authorities about the spread of a new deadly virus and extremely strict anti-epidemic measures may have prevented the SARS-CoV-2 from widely circulating around North Korea until spring 2022 when Pyongyang announced its first large COVID-19 outbreak.[27] Even though we may question the veracity of case numbers and the death toll provided by the North Korean authorities – the caseloads may have been underreported but also "inflated" to make declaring victory over the virus easier – as a result of the self-imposed two-and-half year blockade, the DPRK has insulated itself more than any sanctions would have done.

Although the DPRK is classified as a low-income economy eligible for participation in the COVAX mechanism that it had joined, it has so far refused to accept free supplies of vaccines, including from South Korea, partly because of fears of a lack of efficacy (Sinovac vaccines) and side effects (Astra Zeneca) and partly due to Pyongyang's concerns over 'pre-monitoring" of vaccine delivery. However, as Tomas Ojea Quintana, UN special rapporteur on human rights in the DPRK, highlighted in February 2022,[28] instead of sending shots that would be enough for about 20% of North Korean population as COVAX does, international community should provide North Korea with at least 60 million doses to cover 100% of North Koreans to avoid a humanitarian disaster due to its sealed-off borders.

Despite some initial doubts, Pyongyang has sufficient capabilities to go ahead with a quick rollout of SARS-CoV-2 vaccines,[29] including those requiring a cold chain storage, as previous inoculation campaigns, such as against measles, indicate. Even though Pyongyang would have been more enthusiastic about easing of sanctions to mitigate the economic effects of the country's complete isolation, it may eventually welcome COVID-19 vaccines via an international instrument in order to be able to open up its closed borders and restart a limited trade. The North Korean leadership may favor this route rather than being dependent on its neighbours, China and Russia, for its inoculation stocks and rather than waiting for these bordering countries to get their pandemic under control on their territories first. If Europe (and South Korea) can get involved in this humanitarian aid, this type of COVID-19 assistance to the DPRK via COVAX and/or other international instruments could advance the inter-Korean relations and amplify the EU's weight on the Korean peninsula and Asia more broadly.

Connecting Digitally Europe and South Korea

Although the EU and ROK have tremendously benefitted from their free trade agreement (FTA) and the FTA has become a template for future EU trade deals with Japan, Canada, Singapore, etc., there are various policy areas where Brussels and Seoul could expand their economic cooperation. Thanks to being exposed to the Sino-American rivalry, galvanizing coordination on 5G networks, semi-conductor production and other aspects of digitalization could become one of the long-term priorities (coupled with short-term actions) for Brussels and Seoul.

Since the conflict over China's Huawei and its safety is one of the hottest points of contention between the US and China, building together reliable 5G networks without annoying one or the other power could be a key achievement between the like-minded partners – a long-term goal encompassing both digitalization and national security. Because of dangers posed by North Korea, the South cannot afford to lose trust and information sharing with Washington as former Secretary of State Pompeo once insinuated[30] when warning against the use of Huawei in their telecom infrastructure. Furthermore, Seoul does not want to provoke the Chinese into another trade and tourism boycott as it had happened when the Blue House under President Park Geun-hye allowed the deployment of the US-made THAAD anti-ballistic missile system.[31]

In a similar vein, the Europeans have been for some time grappling with the question of whether or not (and where) to allow Huawei into their next generation digital equipment. Even though the EU has agreed on a specific toolbox[32] to measure cybersecurity risks, the final decision is up to each EU Member State. Germany still has to make up its mind. Yet if the EU and South Korea were to agree on an enhanced cooperation in the digital field, it would put them in a good stead vis-à-vis the American and Chinese pressures, particularly if Samsung and Nokia/Ericsson were to team up rather than compete.

Connecting the European and South Korean Fights Against Climate Change

Apart from digitalization, there is even a greater complementarity of views between Brussels and Seoul on climate change. Seoul's Green new deal[33] fits with the European green deal.[34] Despite concerns about implementation, Beijing has also moved towards the "greener" side with President Xi's promise of China becoming carbon-neutral by 2060. In contrast to Donald Trump's aversion to any climate talks and the Paris Accord, Joe Biden's revamped clean energy and environmental justice plan[35] also overlaps with the European, South Korean (and Chinese) plans. As noted earlier, Biden has already brought the US back under the Paris Agreement. This opens the path to a good prospect for a more extensive quadrilateral cooperation that could bring closer together Brussels, Seoul, Beijing and Washington, at least in one policy area.

Fighting climate change might also be an efficient way of bringing North Korea into the international fold. Involving the DPRK officials in various "green deal" negotiations might be a good way of having discussions on a less controversial subject than denuclearization. Sitting around the same negotiating table and debating an issue of concern for all the parties can create mutual trust and learning from one another. It would also be beneficial for the North Koreans to get more information on, and actual assistance in, building tidal and wind power in addition to developing the nuclear. Such a climate dialogue could also improve the inter-Korean relations: after all, it was Pyongyang which ratified and entered into force of the Paris Accord a few months earlier than Seoul did.

There are some indications that the North Korean side could be open to this. Despite its reluctance to send diplomats in person to any international venues due to COVID-19 concerns, DPRK's London-based Ambassador Choe Il attended the COP26 multilateral climate conference in Glasgow in October 2021.[36] This was one of very rare occasions – perhaps apart from the UN – when a North Korean envoy was present. Moreover, Ambassador Choe was in the room when South Korean President Moon gave his speech on the possible forestry cooperation with the DPRK.

Even denuclearization could be tackled through the prism of preserving the nature. Instead of dismantling the Yongbyon nuclear reactor and other similar facilities, the deliberations could refocus on how to keep them safe in order to avoid disasters like in Fukushima or Chernobyl. Any catastrophe would affect all the neighbouring countries, such as South Korea, China, Japan and beyond. Nuclear safety should be in everyone's interest, including the staunchest critics of Pyongyang: capitals equipped with the necessary knowledge and manpower, like Paris, Tokyo and Washington, could share lessons on how to prevent – and how (not) to cope with – a nuclear accident. As with procuring COVID-19 vaccines through an international mechanism, talking nuclear safety within a global forum where the DPRK is viewed as an equal player might be a good training ground for other, more difficult, negotiations.

Such a rosy scenario may however not materialize. Natural disasters like floods and typhoons may keep striking the DPRK countryside, while North Korea may indeed decide to procure, officially or surreptitiously, some amount of the SARS-CoV-2 vaccines for the elites as well as the basic necessities from its closest neighbor, China, while leaving the remaining population vulnerable. Insulated from the outside world by a COVID-19-related shutdown more so than by any sanctions, and without any substantive contacts with South Korea, Pyongyang may be tempted to not just show off, but to actually try out its latest massive ICBM weapon.[37]

However, in the era of the heightened Sino-American competition, instead of the international community rallying behind a US-led "maximum pressure 2.0", Beijing (and Moscow) will not want to give up on North Korea as its political buffer zone while doing its utmost to keep it economically afloat.[38] Moreover, with the human rights situation deteriorating within China itself, a new Sino-North Korean kinship might be developing. As an ordinary Chinese was quoted to having said: "We used to think North Korea was our past – now we realize it's our future."[39]

To avoid an uneasy choice which of the two policies – more pressure and sanctions, or more engagement – towards the DPRK to pursue, Seoul and Brussels may now have the last chance to prevent North Korea from becoming yet another theater for disagreements between Beijing and Washington – and to stop it from slipping completely into the Chinese orbit.[40] The EU has always claimed that it needs to be asked by the relevant parties to get engaged on the Korean peninsula affairs. President Moon's call for the EU to "play a big role"[41] at the EU-South Korea summit in June 2020 did just that. It is now up to the EU to respond appropriately, revamp its policy towards the DPRK[42] and work closely with its South Korean partner to draft proposals that could help resolve the North Korean conundrum without alienating either Washington, or Beijing – or, indeed, Pyongyang.

Strengthening the Strategic Partnership, Creating a Network of Like-Minded Allies: How to Connect Better Europe and South Korea within the US-China Conflict

2020 should have been the year when the two Koreas could have, ideally together rather than separately, commemorated the 70th anniversary of the beginning of the Korean War. Declaring the end to that war would have been a success. Yet the COVID-19 pandemic eclipsed any such efforts. This anniversary was not only instrumentalized by the two Koreas but also by China. When visiting an exhibition in honor of the Chinese People's Volunteers forces entering the war, President Xi Jinping portrayed this action as the "historic and resolute decision"[43] of the Chinese Communist Party to resist the American aggression. Instead of calling for peace, China's top leader deftly used the opportunity to call for yet another – albeit so far cold – war with the US.

With the Russian invasion of Ukraine unfolding in front of our eyes, President Xi's remarks clearly indicate where things are headed in the near future: the Sino-American rivalry will encroach on other areas. Europe should take this Korean experience as a serious warning. How can Brussels and Seoul navigate the contest between the US and China that had started under the Obama Presidency, if not earlier, was clearly visible during the Trump Presidency, and has deepened since Joe Biden took office?

This chapter argued that the EU and ROK should, first and foremost, strengthen their mutual Strategic Partnership in a number of areas: health, digital connectivity and climate change. Secondly, Brussels and Seoul should try to identify areas where they can pre-empt, or at least manage, the rivalry between Beijing and Washington from escalating (such as in the case of North Korea). Last but not least, the EU and ROK should explore whether there are any other like-minded partners, especially in the Indo-Pacific, that are reluctantly siding with either the US or with China but would prefer teaming up with the EU and South Korea.

The ASEAN countries come quickly to mind: the EU has become a "networked" power through its numerous concluded (or under negotiation) FTAs with ASEAN members and has been a large contributor to the (post)-pandemic aid and recovery in the region. Similarly, President Moon's New Southern Policy serves an analogous purpose of joining up with ASEAN to create a network of friends supporting the reconciliation on the Korean peninsula.

A good case could also be made for an enhanced collaboration with Canada, Australia and New Zealand. Should such a strategy work, the EU could upgrade and expand its standing in the Indo-Pacific, while ROK might get a better chance solving the inter-Korean issues. Brussels and Seoul may soon discover that finding together like-minded allies happy to join up forces can prove to be the most effective strategy. Most of all, such an enhanced cooperation can help reviving multilateralism and a rules-based order across the globe. Such a policy will benefit us all.

---

1 Josep Borrell, "Opening remarks to the annual German Ambassadors' Conference", EEAS, May 25, 2020, https://eeas.europa.eu/headquarters/headquarters-homepage/79817/annual-german-ambassadors'-conference-2020-opening-remarks-high-representative-vice-president_en.

2 European External Action Service, "EU Global Strategy," accessed August 27, 2022, https://eeas.europa.eu/topics/eu-global-strategy_en.

3 Richard Haas, "Trump's foreign policy doctrine? The withdrawal doctrine," *Washington Post*, May 27, 2020, https://www.washingtonpost.com/opinions/2020/05/27/trumps-foreign-policy-doctrine-withdrawal-doctrine/.

4 Joe Biden, "Remarks by President Biden on America's Place in the World", The White House, February 4, 2021, https://www.whitehouse.gov/briefing-room/speeches-remarks/2021/02/04/remarks-by-president-biden-on-americas-place-in-the-world/.

5 "Aukus: UK, US and Australia launch pact to counter China," *BBC News*, September 16, 2021, https://www.bbc.com/news/world-58564837.

6 Cited in "Aukus: China denounces US-UK-Australia pact as irresponsible", *BBC News*, September 17, 2021, https://www.bbc.com/news/world-58582573.

7 Danielle Haynes, "Top EU leader Charles Michel calls for 'transparency' after AUKUS sub deal", *UPI*, September 24, 2021, https://www.upi.com/Top_News/US/2021/09/24/eu-charles-michel-general-assembly/9801632503805/.

8 Ania Nussbaum, "France Drops Australia From List of Key Indo-Pacific Partners", *Bloomberg*, February 22, 2022, https://www.bloomberg.com/news/articles/2022-02-22/france-drops-australia-from-list-of-key-indo-pacific-partners.

9 For the quote, see e.g. Kori Schake and Erica Pepe, "70 Years of NATO: The Strength of the Past, Looking into the Future", ETH Zurich, May 6, 2019, https://css.ethz.ch/en/services/digital-library/articles/article.html/1097618a-96c9-45b2-89f7-092198f84a7c.

10 Nathan Vanderklippe, "Michael Kovrig and Michael Spavor mark 600 days in detention in China," *The Globe and Mail*, July 31, 2020, https://www.theglobeandmail.com/world/article-600-days-in-detention-a-sobering-milestone-for-michael-kovrig/.

11 See e.g. "China spy suspect casts chill over EU's vulnerabilities", *Financial Times*, 2020, https://www.ft.com/content/02921486-3e97-11ea-b232-000f4477fbca.

12 Ben Blanchard and Yew Lun Tian, "Czech senate speaker will pay 'heavy price' for Taiwan visit, China says", *Reuters*, August 31, 2020, https://www.reuters.com/article/us-taiwan-czech-china-idUSKBN25R059.

13 "Prague must show goodwill to mend market confidence", *Global Times*, September 6, 2020, https://www.globaltimes.cn/content/1200059.shtml.

14 "China halts Lithuania beef, dairy and beer imports amid Taiwan row", *BBC News*, February 11, 2022, https://www.bbc.com/news/business-60343316.

15 European Commission, "EU refers China to the WTO following its trade restrictions on Lithuania", Press Release, European Commission, January 27, 2022, https://trade.ec.europa.eu/doclib/press/index.cfm?id=2355.

16 "BTS in trouble in China over Korean War comments", *BBC News*, October 13, 2020, https://www.bbc.com/news/world-asia-54513408.

17 "Samsung removes BTS-related products from China's e-commerce stores after the band angered netizens", *Global Times*, October 12, 2020, https://www.globaltimes.cn/content/1203171.shtml.

18 Jasmine Turner, "China's Foreign Affairs Deputy Director Speaks Up On The Recent BTS Controversy With China... Chinese Netizens Are Not Appeased", *Koreaboo*, October 12, 2020, https://www.koreaboo.com/news/bts-controversy-china-foreign-affairs-deputy-director/.

19 "Is South Korea Again Becoming a Shrimp Among Whales?", *Hankyoreh*, July 30, 2015, http://english.hani.co.kr/arti/english_edition/english_editorials/702458.html.

20 Laura Bicker, "Coronavirus in South Korea: How 'trace, test and treat' may be saving lives", *BBC News*, March 12, 2020, https://www.bbc.com/news/world-asia-51836898.

21 Council of the EU, "Council agrees to start lifting travel restrictions for residents of some third countries", Press Release, Council of the EU, June 30, 2020, https://www.consilium.europa.eu/en/press/press-releases/2020/06/30/council-agrees-to-start-lifting-travel-restrictions-for-residents-of-some-third-countries/.

22 "Fund Raised, Coronavirus Global Response, accessed August 21, 2022, https://global-response.europa.eu/pledge_cs.

23 "Commitment agreements", COVAX, October 12, 2020, https://www.gavi.org/sites/default/files/covid/pr/COVAX_CA_COIP_List_COVAX_PR_12-10.pdf.

24 Sangmi Cha, "South Korea to secure coronavirus vaccines for 60% of population", *Reuters*, September 15, 2020, https://www.reuters.com/article/us-health-coronavirus-southkorea-vaccine-idUSKBN26605X.

25 Tereza Novotna, Korea and The EU Battling Covid19: Towards Cooperation to Improve the Global Governance of Health? Asia Trends, Paris, Vol.7, Fall 2021, pp. 116-128 https://asiacentre.eu/fr/2021/09/13/at7/.

26 The DPRK announced its first ban on foreigners entering the country two days before Wuhan, China went into lockdown, on 23 January 2020.

27 For an overview of the COVID-19 outbreak in the DPRK, see "Coronavirus in North Korea: COVID-19 Tracker", NK News, accessed August 22, 2022, https://www.nknews.org/pro/coronavirus-in-north-korea-tracker/.

28 Josh Smith, World should send 60 mln COVID-19 vaccines to N.Korea, U.N. investigator says, *Reuters*, February 23, 2022, https://www.reuters.com/world/asia-pacific/world-should-send-60-mln-COVID-19-vaccines-nkorea-un-investigator-says-2022-02-23/.

29 Nagi M. Shafik. C. Yoonhee Ryder and Kee B. Park, "North Korea's Vaccination Capabilities: Implications for a COVID-19 Campaign," *38 North*, August 5, 2021, https://www.38north.org/2021/08/north-koreas-vaccination-capabilities-implications-for-a-COVID-19-campaign/.

30 David Brunnstrom, "Pompeo tells Germany: Use Huawei and lose access to our data", *Reuters*, May 31, 2019, https://www.reuters.com/article/us-usa-germany-idUSKCN1T10HH.

31 John Hemmings and Sungmin Cho, "South Korea's Growing 5G Dilemma," CSIS, July 2020, https://www.csis.org/analysis/south-koreas-growing-5g-dilemma.

32 European Commission, "Cybersecurity of 5G networks - EU Toolbox of risk mitigating measures," European Commission, 29 January 2020, https://digital-strategy.ec.europa.eu/en/library/cybersecurity-5g-networks-eu-toolbox-risk-mitigating-measures.

33 David Vetter, "South Korea Embraces EU-Style Green Deal For COVID-19 Recovery", *Forbes*, April 16, 2020, https://www.forbes.com/sites/davidrvetter/2020/04/16/south-korea-embraces-eu-style-green-deal-for-COVID-19-recovery/?sh=16c95bf65611.

34 "A European Green Deal", European Commission, accessed 20 August 2022, https://ec.europa.eu/info/strategy/priorities-2019-2024/european-green-deal_en.

35 "The Biden Plan for a Clean Energy Revolution and Environmental Justice", Biden-Harris, accessed August 27, 2022, https://joebiden.com/climate-plan/.

36 Chaewon Chung, „North Korean ambassador to UK attends UN climate conference in Glasgow", *NK News*, November 2, 2021, https://www.nknews.org/2021/11/north-korean-ambassador-to-uk-attends-un-climate-conference-in-glasgow/.

37 "North Korea displays 'massive' ICBM at military parade," *BBC News*, October 10, 2020, https://www.

bbc.com/news/world-asia-54491657.

38 Andrei Lankov, „Growing US-China tensions could keep North and South Korea apart forever", *NK News*, October 16, 2020, https://www.nknews.org/2020/10/as-us-china-tensions-grow-korean-unification-may-be-prolonged-indefinitely/.

39 Anna Fifield, "As repression mounts, China under Xi Jinping feels increasingly like North Korea,", *Washington Post*, September 28, 2020, https://www.washingtonpost.com/world/asia_pacific/china-muslims-xinjiang-north-korea-repression/2020/09/28/ad2fefd8-f316-11ea-8025-5d3489768ac8_story.html

40 Tereza Novotna, "What Can a New 'Geopolitical' EU Do about North Korea?" *38 North*, February 6, 2020, https://www.38north.org/2020/02/tnovotna020620/.

41 Tereza Novotna, Health, Trade and North Korea: The EU-South Korea Summit and Future Ties, *9DashLine*, July 11, 2020, https://www.9dashline.com/article/health-trade-and-pyongyang-the-eu-south-korea-summit.

42 See Alessandro Ford and Tereza Novotna, Donald Trump and Kim Jong-un need the European Union (with Alessandro Ford), *The Bulletin of the Atomic Scientists*, May 3, 2019 https://thebulletin.org/2019/05/donald-trump-and-kim-jong-un-need-the-european-union/.

43 Xu Wei, „Xi hails victory 7 decades ago", *China Daily*, October 20, 2020 http://www.chinadaily.com.cn/a/202010/20/WS5f8e1c70a31024ad0ba7fa67_1.html.

Promoting Global Value Chain in Europe and East Asia and Role of Free Trade Agreements

Yoo-Duk Kang

Introduction

The expansion and deepening of global value chains (GVCs) has underpinned international trade growth in recent decades. In this process, it has been increasingly crucial to maintain low production costs securing relevant quality at the firm level. GVCs have increased efficiencies and reduced costs, which has led to increased wages and job opportunities for workers, firms, and countries. Many empirical works have shown that GVCs generate considerable economic gains for participating firms and countries that host GVC activities (OECD 2013). Since 2000, the value of intermediate goods traded globally has tripled to more than 10 trillion US dollars per year (Lund *et al.* 2020).

On the other hand, many countries have been experiencing strains in their supply chains amid the US-China competition and the COVID-19 pandemic. As US-China relations have become increasingly strained, the term 'decoupling' has frequently been mentioned in the US and China. A decoupling of the US and Chinese economies would trigger the restructuring of existing GVCs that had allowed the rapid growth of international trade (Wu *et al.* 2021). The disruption in the supply chains of a few essential items and shortage of medical goods during the COVID-19 pandemic already highlighted how countries are interconnected through GVCs. This renewed the debate on the cost and benefits of globalized supply chains. More specifically, recent discussions emphasize the vulnerability associated with fragmentation of production under globalization. As a result, there has been a growing perception that non-economic risks should be considered in operating the supply chain, and several countries, including the US, Europe, and China, are reconsidering reorganizing their supply chain for critical industries.

Although they are not full-scale reconstruction, the current plans to reshuffle supply chains are driven by strategic competition between countries rather than economic calculation at firm levels. The US-China trade dispute being in full swing during the Trump administration has been developing into competition in technology and strategic rivalry. Examples are the Indo-Pacific Alliance, Quad, AUKUS, and the increasing tension in cross-strait relation regarding Taiwan. These divisions result from competitions to secure technological hegemony and leadership in international politics beyond trade interests.

This situation brings about a new challenge in the trade connectivity between Europe and East Asia. Both regions are closely linked by trade-investment. The EU (the UK included) accounts for 21% of the global economy and 34% of total global trade (intra-EU trade included). East Asia is one of the triangular poles in the global economies, representing 28% of global GDP and 25% of global trade. Bilateral trade and investment have been increasing over the last decades on an unprecedented scale. Against this new challenge and realities, this chapter tries to identify trade density between Europe and East Asia, identifying their trade links based on GVCs. It also aims to review the EU's trade policy vis-à-vis East Asian countries from the GVC approach and develop arguments to secure trade connectivity between Europe and East Asia.

Development of GVCs in Europe

Academics and policymakers often conceptualize regional economic integration from European experiences. The EU's longevity and development in advanced economic integration led policymakers and researchers to attempt to draw some conclusions to apply to successful integration in their regions. When the regionalization in East Asia and North America accelerated in the 1970s and 1980s, more than 60% of the total trade of European countries took place between them, namely intra-EU trade. In this context, discussions on the cross-border industrial value chain between companies began earlier in Europe than in any other regions. Non-tariff barriers between countries considerably lowered in completing the Single Market in the 1980s, which created a favorable environment for exchanging intermediate goods between European countries. The four freedom of movement (goods, services, capital, labor) and mutual recognition of regulations have created a seamless intra-EU

Figure 1. Decomposition of production activities

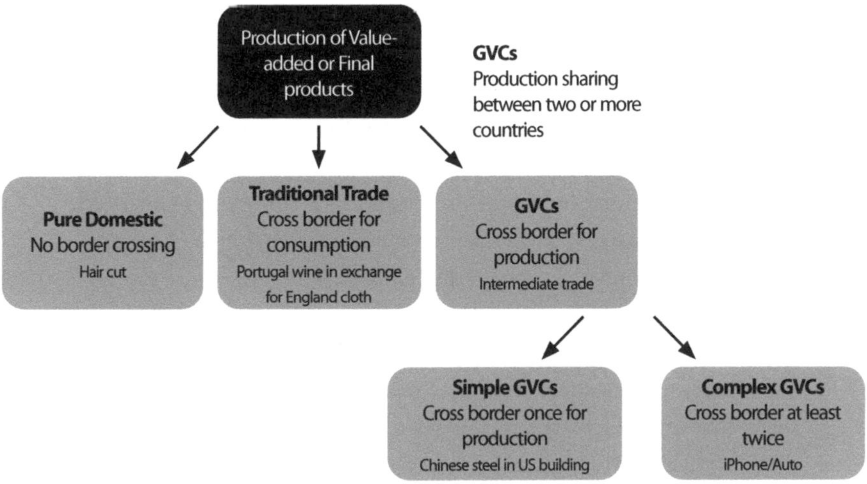

Source: Li, Xin Bo, Meng, and Zhi Wang : Recent patterns of global production and GVC participation, WTO 2019.

trade condition suitable for exploring cross-border industrial networks in Europe. Central and Eastern European countries' accession in the early 2000s also was a catalyst to nurture the coss-European industrial value chains. On the other hand, many factors push European companies to find their industrial partners beyond Europe and extend their supply chains to other regions in the trade and investment liberalization in the 1990s. The emerging countries, particularly in East Asia, became increasingly important in EU's GVCs.

The value chain describes the full range of activities that firms and workers do to bring a product from its conception to its end-use. This includes design, production, marketing, distribution, and support to the final consumer. The activities that comprise a value chain can be contained within a single firm (country) or divided among different firms (countries). Value chain activities can produce goods or services and can be contained within a single geographical location or spread over more expansive areas. GVCs are value chains that can be divided among multiple firms and spread across a wide geographic space.

The GVC approach concentrates on how different tasks, activities and types of operations positioned in the value chain are distributed across locations. Higher volumes of intermediate products such as parts, components, and intermediate services are being produced in stages or processes across different countries and then exported to other countries for further production. Today almost 60% of trade in goods is in intermediates, and the average import content of exports is around 40% (Lamy 2013). Given the increasing complexity and sophistication in GVCs, it has been challenging to identify who produces what kind of value for whom by what kind of activity in the chain.

Another phenomenon related to the expansion of GVCs is the international 'servicification' of manufacturing. Service activities have been increasingly associated with manufacturing activities. The trends show that manufacturing industries incorporate service contents in their production process, and it is increasingly essential for a competitive manufacturer to be supported by relevant service industries. They are regarded as a linkage or glue for different tasks in the manufacturing process. Over the several decades, there has been a substantial replacement of domestic services by imported ones, particularly in high-technological sectors (Saggu and Anukoonwattaka, 2015), and this is the main reason why the servicification of manufacturing is highly linked to the expansion of GVCs.

Current status of GVCs in Europe and East Asia

Table 1 shows a different pattern of how each region has been exploring GVCs in their trade. All regions (North America, the EU, and East and Southeast Asia) have a high proportion of final demand through regional value production, and the EU has the highest proportion in the automobile sector, showing that value chains are closely formed between regional neighbors. For example, in the case of North America, 19.7% of automobile production was supplied with added value (intermediate goods) from East Asia in 2015, while the EU's reliance on East Asia was only 8% in the same sector. In the EU, the proportion of value-added supplied from other regions has decreased in computer and electronics, optical products, textiles, and clothing. It is noteworthy that the proportion of procurement from East Asia more than doubled from 12.3% in 2005 to 25.7% in 2015 in textiles and apparels and from 23.0% to 31.3% in computer and electronics. In other words, with the rise of East Asia in industrial production and trade, GVC in the EU and North America shows a pattern of expanding from regional orientations to East Asia, while the EU still maintains a solid level of GVC in the automobile industry.

The overseas production value in exports of European countries is around 30%, which is much higher than the average of G20 countries (less than 20%) or the US and Japan (within 10%). It means that they use GVCs more actively than countries in other regions. China's GVC participation is on the decline in the long run, and the US is also showing a modest decline, while the EU's GVC participation remains the same.

Table 1. Regional demand for selected manufactured goods, 2005 and 2015 (By region of value added origin)

	Region of final demand						
		North America		European Union		East and Southeast Asia	
Computer, electronic and optical products	value added origin	2005	2015	2005	2015	2005	2015
	Intra-regional	61.9	55.3	60.3	51	82.1	83.2
	North America	0	0	9	8.4	7.7	5.9
	European Union	6.2	5.2	0	0	5.6	5.2
	East and Southeast Asia	27.6	35.3	23	31.3	0	0
	Rest of the World	4.3	4.3	7.8	9.3	4.6	5.7
	Region of final demand						
		North America		European Union		East and Southeast Asia	
Motor vehicles	value added origin	2005	2015	2005	2015	2005	2015
	Intra-regional	67.6	64.4	83.2	80.8	86.4	82.6
	North America	0	0	3	3.5	2.8	4
	European Union	11.4	11.3	0	0	5.7	8.3
	East and Southeast Asia	16.6	19.7	7.1	8	0	0
	Rest of the World	4.4	4.6	6.7	7.7	5.1	5.1
	Region of final demand						
		North America		European Union		East and Southeast Asia	
Textiles and apparel	value added origin	2005	2015	2005	2015	2005	2015
	Intra-regional	45.8	32.3	69.8	52.3	85.3	88.3
	North America	0	0	1.9	1.9	2.5	1.8
	European Union	7.8	5.3	0	0	5.7	3.7
	East and Southeast Asia	29.8	46.3	12.3	25.7	0	0
	Rest of the World	16.6	16.1	15.9	20.1	6.5	6.2

Source: OECD, Trade in Value Added (TiVA) database, December 2018

When we focus on the individual country, the small countries (primarily Central and Eastern European Countries) have a higher GVC participation than large countries. This is because they have a manufacturing base fueled by foreign direct investment, motivated by the EU enlargement and overall reshuffle of industrial production in Europe. Germany, France, and the UK, which have relatively large economies among European countries, have low participation in GVC (rear participation), reflecting their production structure or service of the economy. The intra-EU trade share of the CEECs reaches 70-80%, while that of other European countries (EU-15) remains 50-65%. In addition, despite the overall deindustrialization in Europe over the last twenty years, CEECs did not experience this trend significantly. Compared to the United States, China, and Japan, most EU member countries have higher GVC participation.

Figure 2. Foreign value added share of manufactured exports, 2005 and 2015

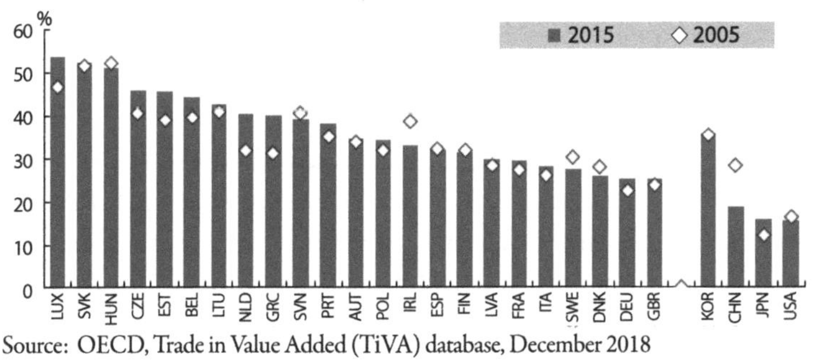

Source: OECD, Trade in Value Added (TiVA) database, December 2018

European countries are more active in integrating intermediate service contents into the manufacturing process. The shares of service contents in manufacturing products are higher in EU member countries than in countries in other regions. In this sense, the overall competitiveness of industrial sectors is highly related to how service sectors can provide high-quality services as intermediate contents. France, Italy, and the UK use more service content from domestic sources, while

Figure 3. Services value added embodied in manufacturing exports, by domestic and foreign origin, 2015

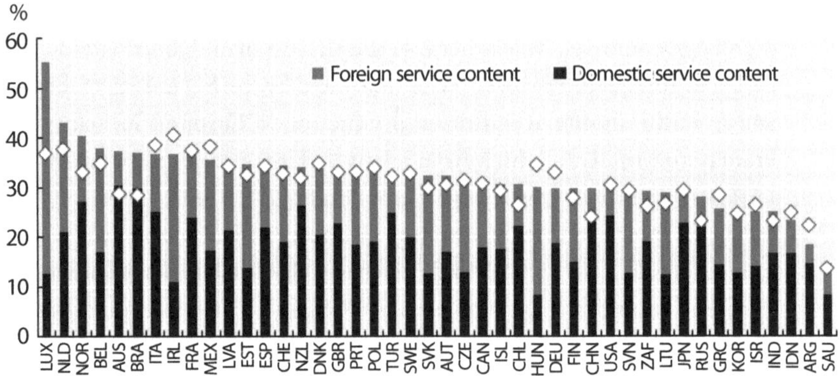

Note: As a percentage of total manufacturing exports.

Source: OECD, Trade in Value Added (TiVA) database, December 2018.

most of CEECs such as Slovakia and the Czech Republic rely on service intermediate from foreign sources.

As the industrial production capacity of East Asian countries increased rapidly, the existing Europe-centered industrial network has been reorganized, connecting to the industrial network in East Asia. Figure 4 illustrates how the industrial network is set up in Europe, focusing on Germany, given that the latter has the most significant manufacturing production and exports. Comparing 2000 and 2017, the industrial structure centered in Germany has been strengthened in Europe, while in China, industrial production and trade surged, resulting in a significant change in Asia's industrial structure, which led to the connection of European industrial networks to East Asia. When we review these networks by sector, China has emerged as a supply hub in the textile industry, while Italy in Europe maintains its position as a supply hub in the region. In information and communication technology (ICT), Japan's role in East Asia declined, but China advanced significantly as an industrial hub in regional value chains. In the service sector, Germany, the UK, France, and the Netherlands are still highly

Figure 3. Services value added embodied in manufacturing exports, by domestic and foreign origin, 2015

(1) All industries

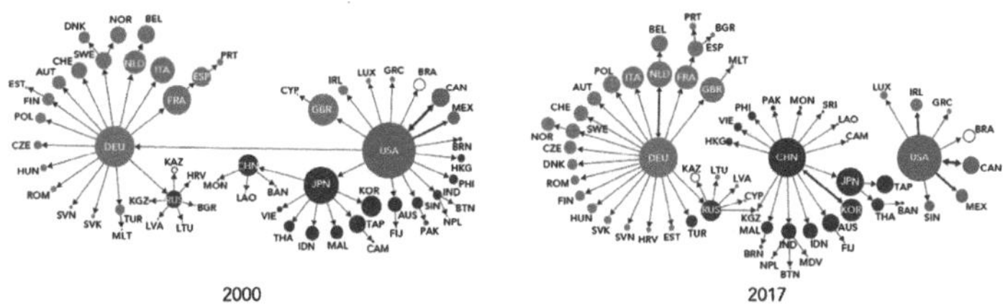

(2) Textiles

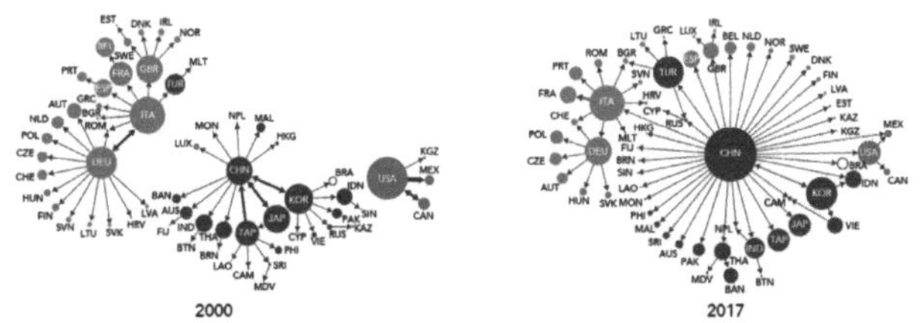

(3) Information, Communication and Technology

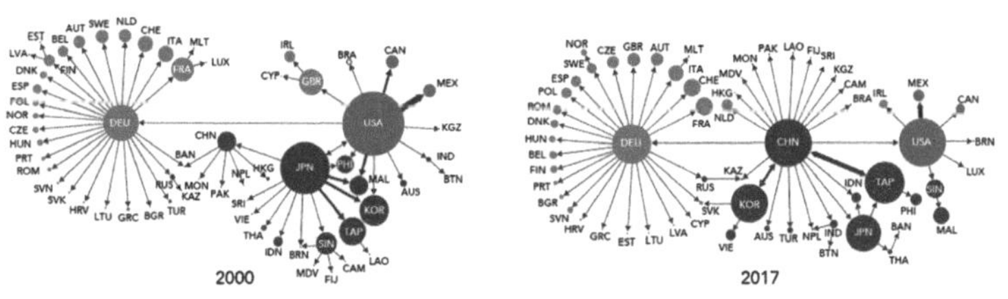

(4) Service

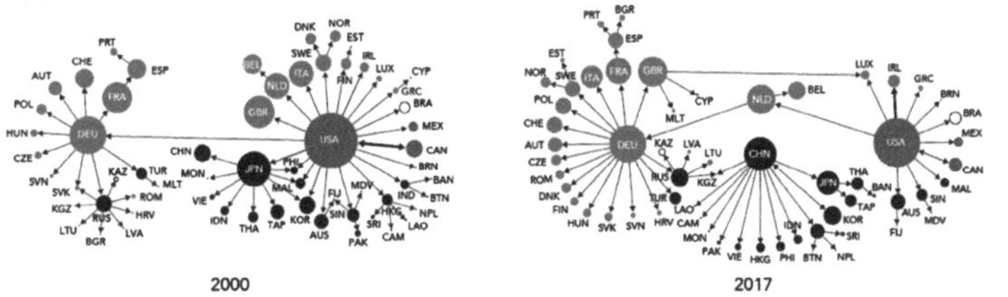

Source: Xin Li, Bo Meng, and Zhi Wang, Recent patterns of global production and GVC participation, In Global Value Chain Development Report 2019 : Technological Innovation, Supply Chain Trade, and Workers in a Globalized World. WTO, 2019, pp. 28~30.

competitive and maintain diversified supply hubs in Europe, and China's role is yet limited.

GVCs and Trade Policy

The spread of GVC tells us an opportunity to expand significant issues of trade policy from tariffs to a wide range of policy areas. The causes of the spread of GVCs in the 2000s include a decrease in transaction and coordination costs due to the development of transportation and ICT, and a global trade liberalization phenomenon. The need for electronic information exchange in the value chain has soared to operate GVC, and the volume of e-commerce has increased dramatically. In particular, in the case of the EU, non-tariff barriers between member states were considerably lowered in completing the European single market. The spread of GVC means that industrial networks between countries are closely intertwined, and trade policies should change from the perspective of mercantilism to support all areas of production and promote a cross-border exchange of goods, services and all tasks, including the movement of labor. In this regard, countries must develop policies to support not only produce parts but also networks across all production industries, such as service, research, design, marketing, assembly, distribution, and service after-sales. In the case of trade policy, its scope has been expanded from tariff issues to regulatory issues (non-tariff barriers), access to raw materials, innovation, IPR protection, etc. As the manufacturing-service industry network strengthens, the competitiveness of the service industry is directly linked to the competitiveness of the manufacturing industry, and service trade in trade policy has more critical place. To operate GVCs in more efficient manner, the following areas became increasingly important; logistics, support, training, insurance, communication, transportation, and business service. In addition, much of the service trade is developed through foreign (or overseas) direct investment, further strengthening investment position

Table 2. FTAs of the EU and the US and 'WTO-extra' provisions

Area covered	Content
Anti-corruption	Regulations concerning criminal offense measures in matters affecting international trade and investment.
Competition policy	Maintenance of measures to proscribe anticompetitive business conduct; harmonization of competition laws; Establishment or maintenance of an independent competition authority.
Consumer protection	Harmonization of consumer protection laws; exchange of information and experts; training.
Data protection	Exchange of information and experts; joint projects.
Movement of capital	Liberalization of capital movement; prohibition of new restrictions.
Labor market regulations	Regulation of the national labor market; affirmation of International Labor Organization (ILO) commitments; enforcement.
Intellectual Property Rights (IPR)	Accession to international treaties not referenced in the TRIPs Agreement.
Approximation of legislation	Application of EC legislation in national legislation.
Audiovisual	Promotion of the industry; encouragement of co-production.
Civil protection	Implementation of harmonized rules.
Innovation policies	Participation in framework programs; promotion of technology transfers.
Cultural cooperation	Promotion of joint initiatives and local culture.

Area covered	Content
Economic policy dialogue	Exchange of ideas and opinions; joint studies.
Education and training	Measures to improve the general level of education.
Energy	Exchange of information; technology transfer; joint studies.
Financial assistance	Set of rules guiding the granting and administration of financial assistance.
Health	Monitoring of diseases; development of health information systems; exchange of information.
Illegal immigration	Conclusion of re-admission agreements; prevention and control of illegal immigration.
Industrial cooperation	Assistance in conducting modernization projects; facilitation and access to credit to finance.
Information society	Exchange of information; dissemination of new technologies; training.
Research and technology	Joint research projects; exchange of researchers; development of public-private partnership.
Taxation	Assistance in conducting fiscal system reforms.

Source: Quoted from Horn *et al.* (2010).

in trade policy. 60% of the EU's overseas investment is linked to service trade.

From an academic and policy point of view, paying more attention to GVCs overlaps with the trend that trade agreements gradually began to include non-traditional issues. The US and EU promoted a comprehensive free trade agreement (FTA), often termed as *deep integration*, and in this process, various issues beyond the existing World Trade Organization (WTO) negotiating agenda began to be included in the trade policy. Many FTAs signed after the mid-2000s include many so-called 'WTO extras' issues, which are discussed in WTO negotiations.

Since the Global Europe initiative in 2006, the EU has pushed for comprehensive FTAs. Since then, several new issues have been increasingly reflected in trade policies. First, the recent trade policy focus on opening the service market. The EU led the negotiations of the Service Trade Agreement (TiSA) and advocated the agreement. All FTAs concluded by the EU since 2006 include service provisions indicating additional concessions based on the GATS concession list. In 2018, the EU ranked first (based on offshore trade), accounting for 25.1% ($1.89 trillion) of global service exports and 20.6% ($8.65 billion) of imports. 2019 (WTO 2019). Since the intra-EU trade accounts for 65% of total trade of the EU, it is estimated that the actual statistics will be much more than the statistics of the WTO that excludes intra-EU trade. In order to promote and support GVC, the EU emphasizes the need to open the service market both in the EU and abroad and focuses on opening the service market of the other country using trade agreements. The EU adheres to the integrated package method that promotes together without separating goods and service agreements in promoting the FTA. The EU also demands that the WTO Environmental Goods Agreement (EGA) address the service sector (European Commission 2015).

Second, the current EU's trade policy emphasizes the role of digital regulations. Free data movement between borders is necessary to maintain European industrial competitiveness and to establish global norms in the field by promoting mutual recognition of IT-related regulations and harmonization of standards. Untransparent principles, the government's interference, and the demand for local data storage is identified as the reasons that hinder EU companies' use of GVC (European Commission 2015).

Third, the EU has been advocating the movement of high skilled workers (not every sector), at least for temporary ones related to goods and equipment, to make the most of the bilateral FTA. Negotiations are promoted so that the product can be treated equally with market access. For example, when European equipment is exported to the oversea market through preferential tariffs and engineering or maintenance services are provided, preferential treatment is secured in the provision of this service.

Forth, the EU tends to maximize its supremacy in global rule-making, strengthening regulatory cooperation with its trade partners. The EU has traditionally implemented a 'regulatory export' policy of EU regulations offshore, and this stance has been explicitly declared in 2010 (European Commission 2010). Efforts to reflect EU regulations abroad are carried out in general and in various fields such as labor and the environment.

EU's FTAs with East Asia

In 2006, the European Commission announced seeking ambitious trade deals with third countries using a bilateral format (European Commission 2006). The communication identified the ASEAN, Korea, and MERCOSUR as "priorities ."India, Russia, and the Gulf Cooperation Council (GCC) members are said to have combinations of market potential and protection levels, making them of direct interest to the EU despite their relatively low profile in FTA policy. The communication recognized China as a substantial developing economy and paid particular attention to China, discussing it separately. China was said to meet economic criteria, but it requires special attention because of the opportunities and risks.

Fifteen years later, the EU concluded trade deals with Korea,

Japan, Singapore, and Vietnam, and other trade deals have been under negotiation. Some of them are suspended.

For India, the EU began FTA negotiations in June 2007, but negotiations have been suspended since May 2013 due to differences in automobile tariffs and pharmaceutical market issues. In negotiating an FTA with India, the EU aimed for a comprehensive FTA beyond the abolition of commodity tariffs and maintains its position to include a sustainable development chapter including labor and environmental provisions. With the suspension of negotiations prolonged, the EU is considering signing a stand-alone investment protection agreement with India.

For Singapore, the EU began negotiations on bilateral FTAs with Singapore in March 2010, concluded negotiations in October 2014, and entered into force in November 2019 due to delays in internal EU procedures. Despite the active positions of the EU and Singapore, it took a long time (5 years) from the conclusion of the negotiations to take effect due to legal disputes within the EU. The reason why it took five years for the EU-Singapore FTA to take effect after the negotiations were that legal lawsuits were filed within the EU and member states over the investment provisions of the FTA. In order to minimize legal controversy, the EU-Singapore trade agreement was signed and entered into force in such a way that two individual agreements (FTA + Investment Protection Agreement) were signed separately. Accordingly, the EU separated the investment protection sector from the FTA and signed the FTA and investment protection agreement (two agreements) with Singapore in October 2018, and the agreement entered into force in November 2019.

The EU and Vietnam began FTA negotiations in June 2012 and signed the agreement in June 2019, and the agreement entered into force in August 2020. Vietnam was very active in promoting trade agreements with the EU, and during the same period, Vietnam participated in TPP negotiations and RCEP to promote a full trade opening. Negotiations are officially underway with Malaysia and Thailand (other countries) but have been pending for a long time.

The FTA signed with Singapore and Vietnam is a comprehensive

FTA that includes components necessary to promote the use of GVC. (Singapore) Due to the nature of Singapore, which applies primarily tariff-free in commodity trade, the EU focused on opening Singapore's service market, and the two sides agreed to open further based on the GATS concession proposal. Singapore opened additionally to European companies in services such as telecommunications, environment, finance, mail, marine transportation, and information technology, and the government procurement market in the environmental and energy sectors was also opened to the EU. The EU allowed Singaporean companies to participate in the EU's railway procurement market. In consideration of the characteristics of ASEAN regional trade, the country of origin standard was relaxed so that when ASEAN member intermediate goods were used, they could be recognized as regional products (Singapore or EU) when certain conditions were met. There was room for pan-ASEAN cumulative origin. The Protocol of Origin stipulates the accumulation of origin throughout much of the first half, especially for 32 items in HS 4 units specified in Annex D; if certain conditions are met, they can be recognized as regional products (Singapore or EU).

Through, Vietnam opened the government procurement market to the EU and abolished or eased its technical standards and customs procedures. The agreement allows accumulation of origin for specific items from offshore, so it is regarded as offshore domestic if certain conditions are met. ◦ Vietnam provides concessions equivalent to those of GPA members to the EU through the WTO's Government Procurement Agreement (GPA) or the FTA. Vietnam will adopt international automotive technical standards for automobiles and parts, abolish Vietnam's unique technical barriers for medicines, and comply with procedures that meet global standards. The EU and Vietnam agreed to cooperate on a high level of labor and environmental protection performance Trade and sustainable development) and to establish an investment protection system through a separate investment protection agreement (IPA).

Concluding remarks

Industrial value chains between Europe and East Asia are dense and complicated, and they reflect trade and investment development over several decades. Some of them have been rectified by bilateral trade deals that focus on stable industrial networks based on GVCs. However, this trade connectivity has been facing serious challenges amid strategic competition between major economies and attempts to redesign supply chains strategically. The Biden administration in the US initiated several executive orders to reinforce supply chains redesign in crucial industries such as semiconductor and electric vehicle batteries. In this attempt, the US government tries to bring back global supply chains to the US to promote more jobs and secure supply chains of the essential industries. China has been developing its attempt to reshuffle industry and trade networks using the so-called 'Dual Circulation' strategy. This is to shield China's economy against global volatility and promote self-reliance while securing its trade relationship with the rest of the world. Facing these attempts of the US and China, the EU has been reorganizing its external policy with the vision of 'Open Strategic Autonomy. It is noteworthy that the EU has been initiating some industrial projects to support European industries. The European Commission supported several industrial projects under the EU's subsidy framework, Important Projects of Common European Interest (IPCEI). This scheme is different from industrial subsidies developed by many countries in several aspects. However, the European Commission tries to secure resilience or reinforce European industries' supply chains in critical sectors.

The discussions so far allow us to spotlight some challenges to existing industrial networks in Europe and Asia and provide implications. First, the EU recognizes that the leadership in the manufacturing sector has shifted to Asia and is moving to reorganize the industrial value chain in Europe. An increasing number of M&A of Chinese firms over European core industries since the global financial crisis and shortage of medical products during the COVID-19 outbreak served as a shift in the perception that the value chain of core technologies or essential goods should be preserved in Europe. However, the EU's supply chain reorganization plan does not have a closed structure, with local corporations of offshore companies (Korea, Japan) also participating. Therefore, it is necessary to actively participate in the EU's industrial policy by utilizing European subsidiaries of Korean companies. Second, the paradigm of technological hegemony is shifting from a technical advantage to a combination of trade policies and environmental regulations. In this transition, there is a perception that gaining the upper hand in the US and Asian countries' purchasing power and technology alone has reached its limit. It aims to secure a non-price/non-technical advantage by applying social regulations (climate, environmental, and human rights) that the EU has strengths to trade policies and corporate supply chains. Therefore, to respond to this, it is necessary to have a competitive edge that combines technology and a regulatory environment by increasing the capacity to accept non-traditional trade issues. Third, the bilateral FTAs that the EU concluded with East Asian countries could be an excellent template to secure the resilience of GVCs connecting two regions. One of the ways is to incorporate bilateral cooperation provisions related to GVCs in the cooperation chapter of the FTAs. To do so, it will be required to identify issues and agendas related to GVCs and develop industry-specific initiatives and discussions on industrial regulation. Once again, the EU's IPCEI may provide a good framework for European firms and East Asian firms that link their industries to European partners.

Bibliography

Anukoonwattaka, Witada., Marco Scagliusi, and Mia Mikic, "Servicification and Industrial Exports from Asia and the Pacific," United Nations ESCAP Trade Insights Issue 10 (2015).

European Commission, Global Europe: Competing in the World, COM(2006) 567 final, (September 2006).

European Commission, Trade, Growth and World Affair: Trade Policy as a Core Component of the EU's 2020 Strategy, COM(2010) 612 (November 2010).

European Commission, Trade for All: Towards a More Responsible Trade and Investment Policy (October 2015).

European Commission, Strategic Plan 2020-2024, Directorate-General for Trade (2020).

European Commission, Trade Policy Review 2021: An Open, Sustainable and Assertive Trade Policy, COM(2021) 66 (February 2021).

Eurostat. https://ec.europa.eu/eurostat/data/database

Lamy, Pascal, Speeches – DG Pascal Lamy, "In value chains, what cannot be counted does not count," March 14, 2013. https://www.wto.org/english/news_e/sppl_e/sppl270_e.htm

Horn, Henrik, Petros C. Mavroidis, and André Sapir, "Beyond the WTO? An anatomy of EU and US preferential trade agreements," The World Economy, Vol. 33, No. 11 (2010), pp. 1565-1588.

Li, Xin Bo, Meng, and Zhi Wang, Recent patterns of global production and GVC participation, In Global Value Chain Development Report 2019 : Technological Innovation, Supply Chain Trade, and Workers in a Globalized World. WTO (2019).

OECD, Interconnected Economies: Benefiting from Global Value Chains, OECD Publishing, Paris (2013).

OECD, Trade in Value Added (TiVA) database (December 2018).

Lund, Susan, James Manyika, Jonathan Woetzel, Edward Barriball, Mekala Krishnan, Knut Alicke, Michael Birshan, Katy George, Sven Smit, Daniel Swan, and Kyle Hutzler, Risk, resilience, and rebalancing in global value chains, McKinsey Global Institute (June 2020).

WTO, World Trade Statistical Review (2019).

WTO, RTA Database, https://rtais.wto.org/UI/charts.aspx

Wu, Jie, Jacob Wood, Xianhai Huang, "How does GVC reconstruction affect economic growth and employment? Analysis of USA–China decoupling," *Asian-Pacific Economic Literature*, Vol. 35, Issue 1 (2021), pp. 67-81.

Examining Europe-China connectivity on trade and investment

The case of the Comprehensive Agreement on Investment (CAI)

Nicola Casarini

Introduction

Trade and investment have traditionally been the driving forces behind Europe-Asia connectivity. Since the mid-1990s, Asian markets have become increasingly important for the EU's global competitiveness and socio-economic welfare position. This was clearly stated by the European Commission in its 2001 Communication on Asia which maintained that 'the EU's role in Asia is to pursue market opening for both goods and services and to overcome obstacles to European trade and investment... [since] active participation for European companies on Asian markets... can contribute to providing qualified jobs for European workers and help the European industry to remain globally competitive'.[1] Back in 1993, the German government had put forward a new strategy towards Asia, advancing the idea that Europe's global competitiveness and economic security would increasingly depend on European companies' capacity to enter into the thriving Asian markets.[2]

Throughout the 1990s, there was a dramatic surge of trade and investment relations between the EU and Asia. At the turn of the millennium, the EU would become Asia's second most important economic partner – behind China, but ahead of the US and Japan.

China has become the cornerstone of Europe's trade relations with Asia. In 2019, Beijing accounted for 11 % in extra-EU exports of goods, becoming the EU's second most important trading partner. Moreover, two-way investments have also surged. To provide a legal framework – currently absent – to their burgeoning economic relations, Brussels and Beijing announced the formal conclusion of the EU-China Comprehensive Agreement on Investment (CAI) at the end of December 2020. If ratified, the CAI would boost trade and investment relations between the EU and China. It would also have profound implications for the United States which is actively working to create a common front with the European allies to counter Beijing's increased self-confidence and assertiveness. Although CAI faces an uncertain future, it was announced only a few weeks before the Biden administration entered into office, as a sign of Europe's determination to promote its 'strategic autonomy' towards Asia.

This chapter focuses on the CAI as an example of the opportunities, and pitfalls, of fostering EU-China connectivity on trade and investment.

EU-China economic connectivity

Economic considerations have traditionally been the main driver of the Sino-European relationship.[3] In 2019, China and the EU traded more than €1.5 billion in goods each day. The EU is now China's most important trading partner, although China ranks number two for the EU, after the US, if both trade in goods and services are considered.

The COVID-19 pandemic which begun in early 2020 led to a strong decline in trade in the first and second quarters of that year. Between the first quarter of 2019 and the second quarter of 2021, the EU's share of imports from China increased by 4%.[4] China's growing share of imports and exports means that in 2021 Beijing overtook the US as the EU's largest trade in goods partner.[5] However, while the EU imported fewer goods from the US, the relationship remains very strong, particularly when services are included in the statistics.[6]

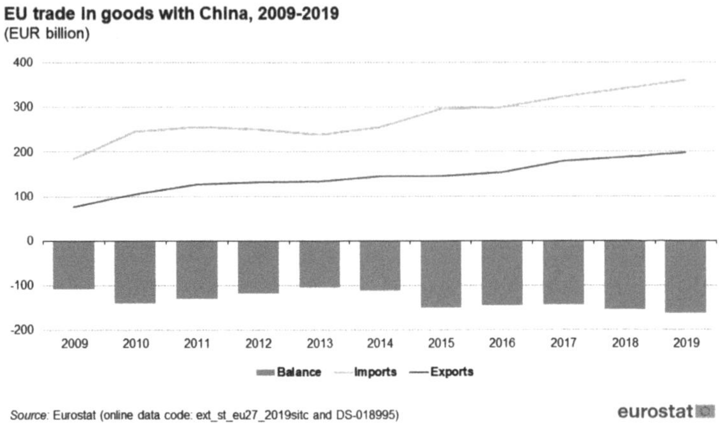

Updated graph (2020/21): https://ec.europa.eu/eurostat/statistics-explained/index.php?title=China-EU_-_international_trade_in_goods_statistics

In recent years, there has been a surge of Chinese investments in the old continent. According to the China Global Investment Tracker, a joint project between the American Enterprise Institute and the Heritage Foundation, China invested nearly $164 billion in Europe between 2005 and 2016. During that same period, it invested $103 billion in the United States. According to the Rhodium Group, a New York based consultancy, Chinese FDI in the EU has increased by almost 50 times in only eight years, from less than $840 million in 2008 to a record high of $42 billion (€35 billion) in 2016. Although Chinese investments in the EU are still comparatively low, they have been evolving rapidly and increasing at unprecedented growth rates.[7]

In the last years, a growing number of scholars and policy makers have begun to argue in favor of more conditionality in EU-China relations, in particular on economic and trade issues.[8] In the same vein, the European Parliament, a number of national Parliaments, and some political forces within EU Member States have stepped up criticism vis-à-vis the Chinese regime and its trade practices, in particular China's lack of reciprocity. Beijing limits foreign investment in its domestic market for almost all sectors. European businesses consistently face difficulties in entering the market, while Chinese companies often receive help from the government, through subsidies or simpler procedures, for example. Foreign companies particularly those with recognised brands and technologically advanced products, are required to share their expertise before they are allowed into the market at all. European investors routinely point out the regulatory and administrative burden that foreign companies have to face in China. While the country is the EU's second largest trading partner, it also has important investment barriers. These include joint venture requirements, market entry restrictions, obligations of technology transfer as well as unjustifiable technical regulations.

China represents a serious economic and trade challenge to Europe, due to its state-dominated economy and its unfair trade practices, which have contributed to de-industrialisation and a declining standard of living across some parts of the old continent - a situation that European countries share with other developed nations, including the United States. Growing imbalances between Europe and China led France, Germany, and Italy to ask the European Commission, in February 2017, to rethink the rules on foreign investment in the EU. This led to the adoption of a screening mechanism which is intended to help the European Commission and the EU member states to evaluate whether a foreign investor is in reality controlled by a third country government.[9] This is clearly aimed at Chinese state-backed enterprises. The screening mechanism makes it more difficult for foreign investors to acquire expertise and technology that could be used to produce goods sold at lower prices. It was a message to Beijing about opening up access to its markets, at a time when the two sides were negotiating the CAI.

In the same vein, the policy paper on China issued by the Federation of German Industries (BDI) in January 2019 - a document which considerably influenced the EU's policy paper on China issued in March 2019 - argued in favour of a more assertive position vis-à-vis Beijing on trade and investment. [10] At the same time, numerous industrial and business associations across Europe continue to be attracted by China's huge domestic market and its expanding middle class which represents a formidable opportunity for many European companies, some of which have shifted production to China to take advantage of lower production costs and global supply chains.

To provide a legal framework to the growing EU-China investment relations, the EU decided to push ahead with the CAI - a landmark agreement on investment reached in principle by Brussels and Beijing on 30 December 2020, after seven years and 35 rounds of negotiations.[11] However, this is not the end of the process which requires actual signature by China and the EU and ratification by the European Parliament. The announcement of the deal triggered an intense debate, as the CAI has found both supporters, but also opponents, inside Europe. It was hailed as a highly beneficial accord for world trade by China, and as a break-through in locking-in China's hitherto opening up and its concessions in the areas of 'market access', 'level playing field' and 'sustainable development' by the European Commission - but met with harsh criticism from the US, where the new Biden administration was not yet inaugurated and saw in it a victory by China in trying to divide the transatlantic allies.

The CAI is currently frozen due to the spat around the situation in Xinjiang, but the debate around it – and the eventuality of its ratification - is far from being over. On 20 May 2021, the European Parliament voted, by an overwhelming majority, to suspend its ratification.[12] The move came after Beijing had imposed retaliatory measures against EU members of Parliament for their support of sanctions against Beijing for its oppression of the Uighur population. The Chinese sanctions imposed in March 2021 on several European entities and political representatives, including five members of the European Parliament and the Subcommittee on Human Rights, were a retaliatory act in response to the EU decision to enact restrictive measures against four Chinese officials over human rights abuses against the Muslim Uyghur minority in the Xinjiang region.[13]

The European Parliament's decision to freeze the CAI reflects growing disenchantment over the past years with China among European lawmakers who – following the sanctions - are determined to stand up more firmly to Beijing. Still, China remains Europe's second largest trading partner and vital engine of world growth, and any moves against Beijing could open the door to escalating economic retaliation - a prospect that may limit how far European governments and the European Commission are willing to go to pressure China. In fact, various EU governments are seeking to resurrect the CAI, since many industrial associations across Europe support the deal, viewing it as an opportunity for European companies to enter and/or acquiring growing shares of the Chinese market.

The debate on CAI

According to the Chinese government, the CAI is the first economic and trade agreement in which China has made commitments in the form of a negative list in all sectors, including services and non-services, demonstrating the country's determination to promote a wider, broader and deeper opening-up to the outside world. In Chinese eyes, the deal intends to further promote China-EU investment cooperation and, consequently, foreign direct investment inflows and outflows. More precisely, the CAI is a very important policy tool to attract FDI by creating a stable and predictable business environment. According to the Chinese Ministry of Commerce, the EU is China's third largest source of FDI and fourth-largest destination for outward FDI in terms of bilateral FDI stocks. The Chinese government views the CAI as a balanced, high-level and mutually beneficial investment agreement. It does not only set up a new legal framework for China-EU economic and trade relations, but also provide stability for China-EU bilateral relations in an uncertain world under major changes.

Some Chinese scholars go even further as they consider CAI as a milestone that could possibly contribute to structural economic and even political changes in China, an aspect generally overlooked or downplayed in European debates. The idea is that the synergies generated by CAI, the domestic socioeconomic changes that it will bring and Chinese leaders' self-consciousness about the necessity of these changes may set the agenda of China's domestic reform, countering thus the predominant view in the West about the slow pace of reform in the country under Xi Jinping.[14]

According to the European Commission, China has made commitments on various points of interest to the EU, including in the form of a negative list in all sectors. This is the main reason why EU officials assert that the agreement is "substantial" (a condition imposed by the EU to close a deal with China). On market access, progress is hard to deny: several sectors are now open to European investors, such as R&D in biological resources, telecommunication/cloud services, international maritime transport, or air transport-related services. By contrast, liberalisation commitments remain limited in agriculture, fisheries, mining, and energy. Also, several constraints imposed so far on European investors, such as quantitative restrictions, equity caps or joint venture requirements, are eliminated in a broader range of sectors (automotive, financial services, computer services, environmental services, or private hospitals in key Chinese cities, among others). This is progress, from a European perspective.

On levelling the playing field, the picture is less rosy: The major commitments relate to the discipline imposed on State-Owned-Enterprises (SOEs), transparency in subsidies, and the elimination of forced technology transfers, though China's track-record in implementation on all these issues raises doubts as to its ability to turn these promises into reality. The CAI makes explicit reference to the integration of environmental sustainability considerations in the bilateral investment relationship (with a reference to the implementation of the Paris Accord on climate change), as well as references to labor standards. The former addition is particularly noteworthy as this is the first time that China has agreed to such ambitious provisions with a trade partner. However, the two sides only commit to facilitating and encouraging investment in environmentally or climate-friendly goods and services generally without further binding provisions. The implementation of CAI – once adopted – will be the real testing ground of all these commitments.

The European business community in China is largely supportive of CAI. Joerg Wuttke, President of the European Union Chamber of

Commerce in China has argued that the CAI makes marginal, though measurable, improvements in market access, recognizing that the biggest gains are the meaningful expansions of the provisions on a level-playing field for the thousands of European companies already in China, while setting a legal foundation at the EU-China level that is currently absent.[15] Representatives of various business associations across Europe see the CAI as an opportunity to outcompete US companies in the Chinese market. The deal may also allow the Chinese government to counter the shopping list contained in the US-China 'phase one' deal negotiated under Trump and maintained by the Biden administration. With the CAI, the EU applies multilateralism and WTO rules, in stark contrast to Trump's trade deal imposed on China invoking 'national security' considerations.

Inside Europe, the main proponents and drivers of the deal have been former German Chancellor Angela Merkel and French President Emmanuel Macron. The latter had originally hoped to seal the deal with pomp by hosting Xi Jinping in Paris during France's Presidency of the European Council in the first half of 2022. Following the Chinese sanctions and the freezing of the deal, both Germany and France have taken a step back, though their hopes about resurrection of the CAI have not disappeared. On 1 April 2022, during the 23rd bilateral Summit between the EU and China, the two sides called for the ratification of their frozen investment agreement "as soon as possible".

Debate about CAI within EU member states has been uneven. In a few countries, some voices have raised concerns about the content of the deal and its timing, while in others the CAI has gone largely unnoticed. Overall, the EU member states' stance on CAI reflects their general policy towards China. In the last years, the majority of member states' attitude towards Beijing has hardened, due to China's growing assertiveness and diminished prospect for the country's liberalisation process. Furthermore, EU member states' positions on CAI are not only dictated by their relationships with Beijing, but also by their level of strategic closeness and cooperation with the United States.

To be ratified, the CAI needs unanimous support from EU

member states and a favourable vote by the European Parliament. In mid-July 2021, the European Parliament underlined the conditions to be met before the legislative gives its consent to the CAI. The conditions are listed in a report prepared by the foreign affairs committee of the European Parliament which calls for using the CAI as a leverage instrument to improve the protection of human rights and support for civil society in China.[16] The pre-ratification commitments listed in the report include a timetable for China's ratification and implementation of key labour laws and concrete measures towards putting an end to human rights violations against the Uyghur minority in the country. It also demands a recommitment by China to uphold its international commitments to Hong Kong. Moreover, the report takes into consideration the new transatlantic climate on China made possible by the arrival of the Biden administration.[17]

In addition to criticizing China, lawmakers have also urged the EU to step up relations with Taiwan – the island country sitting at the junction of the East and South China Seas - that Beijing claims to own under the 'One-China' principle. On 21 October 2021, the European Parliament adopted a *Recommendation* to the Vice-President of the Commission/High Representative of the Union for Foreign Affairs and Security Policy on EU-Taiwan political relations and cooperation. Adopted by a majority of 580 MEPs, with 26 against and 66 abstentions, the document underlines the urgent need to launch an 'impact assessment, public consultation and scoping exercise' for an EU-Taiwan Bilateral Investment Agreement (BIA). The report also expresses grave concern over China's continued military belligerence, pressure, assault exercises, airspace violations and disinformation campaigns against Taiwan, urging the EU to do more to address these tensions, to protect Taiwan's democracy, and the island's status as an important EU partner.[18]

Besides the question of Taiwan, since early 2022 there has been a surge of negative attitudes towards Beijing across Europe – a dynamic that could delay ratification of CAI. Following Russia's invasion of Ukraine, the main opposition to the EU-China investment deal is now coming from Central and Eastern European (CEE) countries with which China has worked in the past to strengthen ties through its Belt and Road Initiative. Some of these countries have begun changing their stance toward Beijing, finding that the economic benefits coming from China is not as great as they had expected. Lithuania, in particular, has been increasingly critical of China. At the end of 2021, the Baltic state set up a representative office in Vilnius that carries the name Taiwan. This triggered Beijing's campaign of economic coercion against the Baltic state. As a response, the EU brought the case to the WTO, hoping to solve the Lithuanian crisis through dialogue with China.

China's retaliation against Vilnius was also in response to the Baltic state's pulling out of the 17+1 grouping – a China-led format founded in 2012 in Budapest with an aim to expand cooperation between Beijing and CEE countries. Lithuania is not alone, as Slovenia and the Czech Republic have also voiced criticism of China and strengthened relations with Taiwan in the first months of 2022. In addition, some political forces in Western Europe have also stepped-up criticism of Beijing, demanding that CAI remains frozen for the foreseeable future.

Conclusion

The ratification of CAI remains in the balance. The initiatives taken by the MEPs in 2021 are in line with the long-standing tradition by the European Parliament to take positions more critical of China than other EU institutions - such as the European Commission and the European External Action Service (EEAS) - as well as EU member states which tend to seek compromise with China for fear of retaliation. It also demonstrates how Europe continues to be split on its China policy: both within – i.e., among EU member states and between EU institutions – as well as on the outside, since Brussels continues to oscillate between closer cooperation with the US on Beijing-related challenges and the pull of the Chinese market.

The more principled position of the European Parliament raises an important question: how far can Europe's connectivity with China on trade and investment go, considering that the human rights' situation inside the Asian giant is not only worsening, but Beijing is now exporting its authoritarian model around the world? The critical position of the European Parliament on the EU-China investment deal coupled with growing opposition to it coming from Lithuania and other Central and Eastern European (CEE) countries seem to be advocating a temporary halt to EU-China connectivity, sharing some similarities with the United States which is intent on decoupling from Beijing. It remains to be seen whether a more principled stance will prevail in Europe, thus leading the old continent to reduce ties with China - or whether Brussels will continue to engage Beijing and eventually ratify the CAI.

---

1 European Commission, *Europe and Asia: A Strategic Framework for Enhanced Partnership*, Brussels: COM (01) 469 final, 4 September 2001, p. 4.

2 Government of the Federal Republic of Germany, *Asien Konzept der Bundesregierung*, Berlin, 25 October 1993.

3 John Farnell and Paul Irwin Crookes, *The Politics of EU-China Economic Relations: An Uneasy Partnership* (Basingstoke: Palgrave, 2016).

4 European Commission - https://ec.europa.eu/trade/policy/countries-and-regions/countries/china/

5 EU international trade in goods - latest developments, *Eurostat*, September 2021 - https://ec.europa.eu/eurostat/statistics-explained/index.php?title=EU_international_trade_in_goods_-_latest_developments&stable=0&redirect=no#Extra-EU_trade_by_partner:_trade_with_China_drives_recovery_of_imports_and_exports_of_goods

6 Daniel Hamilton, 'No, China is not the EU's top trading partner', *Politico*, 19 February 2021 - https://www.politico.eu/article/china-not-eu-top-trade-partner-us-is/

7 Thilo Hanemann, Mikko Huotari and Agatha Kratz, *Chinese FDI in Europe: 2018 Trends and Impact of New Screening Policies*, Berlin: MERICS Papers on China, 6 March 2019 - https://merics.org/en/report/chinese-fdieurope-2018-trends-and-impact-new-screening-policies

8 Janka Oertel, *The new China consensus: How Europe is growing wary of Beijing*, European Council on Foreign

Relations, Policy Brief, 7 September 2020 - https://ecfr.eu/publication/the_new_china_consensus_how_europe_is_growing_wary_of_beijing/. See also: Roland Vogt (ed.), *Europe and China: Strategic Partners or Rivals?* (Hong Kong: Hong Kong University Press, 2012).

9 European Commission, *Proposal for a Regulation establishing a framework for screening of foreign direct investments into the European Union* (COM/2017/487), September 2017 - https://eur-lex.europa.eu/legalcontent/EN/TXT/?uri=CELEX%3A52017PC0487

10 Federation of German Industries, *China - Partner and Systemic Competitor*, Berlin, January 2019 - https://english.bdi.eu/publication/news/china-partner-and-systemic-competitor/

11 European Commission, *EU and China reach agreement in principle on investment*, 30 December 2020 - https://trade.ec.europa.eu/doclib/press/index.cfm?id=2233

12 European parliament, *MEPs refuse any agreement with China whilst sanctions are in place*, Brussels, 20 May 2021 - https://www.europarl.europa.eu/news/en/press-room/20210517IPR04123/meps-refuse-any-agreement-with-chinawhilst-sanctions-are-in-place

13 European Union, *EU imposes further sanctions over serious violations of human rights around the world*, 22 March 2021 - https://www.consilium.europa.eu/en/press/press-releases/2021/03/22/eu-imposes-further-sanctions-overserious-violations-of-human-rights-around-the-world/

14 Xiaolin Duan and Xinning Song, 'Turning pressure into opportunity: CAI and the future of China's structural reform', *Asia Europe Journal*, June 2021 - https://link.springer.com/article/10.1007/s10308-021-00628-0

15 Joerg Wuttke, 'The EU-China CAI-perspectives from the European business community in China', *Asia Europe Journal*, July 2021 - https://link.springer.com/article/10.1007%2Fs10308-021-00631-5

16 European Parliament, *MEPs set out their vision for a new EU strategy for China*, 15 July 2021 – https://www.europarl.europa.eu/news/en/press-room/20210708IPR08013/meps-set-out-their-vision-for-a-new-eustrategy-for-china

17 European Parliament, *Report on a new EU-China strategy* (2021/2037(INI), 26 July 2021 - https://www.europarl.europa.eu/doceo/document/A-9-2021-0252_EN.html

18 European Parliament, *EU-Taiwan political relations and cooperation* (P9_TA(2021)0431), 21 October 2021 - https://www.europarl.europa.eu/doceo/document/TA-9-2021-0431_EN.pdf

Mobility and Educational Cooperation between Korea and the EU

Bongchul Kim

Introduction

As globalization has stimulated the interaction and integration around the world, international mobility is the most active phenomenon including a variety type of flows such as students, workers, refugees, and others. Educational cooperation, one of the main elements of international cooperation, also has continued to increase compared to the past from different countries and regions and it is conducted in a wide range of categories, including mobility of students and researchers among countries.

International Education cooperation is generally defined as promoting internationalization of higher education that includes the policies and practices undertaken by academic systems and institutions and even individuals to cope with the global academic environment.[1] Through international education cooperation, participating actors can establish and develop partnerships and international cooperation networks between universities, companies, governments, and other organizations. Also, this type of mobility supports students to experience cross-cultural awareness, develop adaptability and tolerance, open-mindedness, an understanding of complex global issues, and learn global citizenship.[2] Furthermore, it highlights academic benefits to participation in mobility, improved career outcomes of students who participate in mobility, and increased civic engagement and public diplomacy.

In this regard, the European Union (EU) is a leading actor in promoting international mobility inside and outside Europe in the field of education. The Erasmus Programme in Europe is the representative programme for cultivating international mobility, promoting educational cooperation among countries. The EU aims to spread its norms and values to the international community in network formation with other countries, and as part of these activities, it supports educational cooperation through Erasmus programme, activities by the European External Action Service (EEAS) and the Education, Audiovisual and Culture Executive Agency (EACEA).

The EU's interest in cooperating with other countries to promote international mobility and educational cooperation is evident through cooperation with Asian regions, especially East Asian countries, which are characterized by significant outward and inward student mobility. The number of international students from East Asian countries has increased over the past 10 years to achieve better-quality of education, but also East Asian countries are major destinations for foreign students who want to study in abroad.[3]

In this context, this paper will examine the EU higher education system and Bologna process represented by the Erasmus programme, examine the educational cooperation between Korea and the EU. After that, in addition to the evaluation of Korea-EU educational cooperation, it will discuss the future direction of Korea-EU educational cooperation in the COVID-19 era.

The EU Mobility and Higher Education System

1. Erasmus Programme

The higher education policy at the EU level is the Erasmus programme (European Community Action Scheme for the Mobility of University Students) and it was set up by the Council Decision (87/327/EEC). The Erasmus programme aimed to contribute to the revitalization of the European economy by improving the quality of education based on human exchanges between higher education institutions and improving the skills and employment capabilities of students in higher education institutions.[4] To be specific, the Erasmus programme set three goals which are, i) the establishment of a university network, ii) financial support for students, iii) recognition of degrees and research periods at the EU level. The Erasmus programme, which began in 1987, is considered one of the most successful common policies in the EU and as of 2017, the 30th anniversary of the programme, the Erasmus programme supported a total of 9 million people including 4.4 million of higher education students.[5] As of May 2021, 27 member states of the EU and six non-member countries, Turkey, North Macedonia, Serbia, Iceland, Liechtenstein, and Norway, were named Programme Countries and therefore participated equally in the Erasmus programme. Accordingly, there are a total of 33 countries operating the Erasmus programme.[6]

In 2004, the Erasmus Mundus programme, created for the purpose of cooperation with external countries, was launched to promote mobility and exchange by promoting the modern education and training system that meets the academic tradition, culture and information age of European higher education institutions.[7] This programme was an implementation strategy to devise a global competitive higher education system as laid down in the Bologna process launched in 1999 and the Lisbon strategy in 2000. The European Commission has launched together with the governments of Australia, Japan, New Zealand and the Republic of Korea a new multi-country call for proposals. As a result, the programme called ICI-ECP (Industrialised Countries Instrument-Education Cooperation Programme) launched from 2008, and total 19 universities in ROK and EU joined the program. Erasmus Mundus was a higher education cooperation with all regions of the world, including the third world. However, cooperation with advanced industrial countries in North America and East Asia has been criticized as very insufficient. In reality, EU higher education institutions require strategic cooperation in advanced industrial countries in North America and East Asia, but joint degree operation was restricted due to different academic and academic systems from higher education institutions in this region.[8]

Erasmus+ (Erasmus Plus) was revamped in combining three parts of education programs, namely Lifelong Learning Programme (LLP), International Higher Education Cooperation, and Youth in Action Programme. Under the Erasmus+, it expanded scholarships and raising age of target group of various programmes such as Comenius, Erasmus Mundus, Leonardo, Tempus, Edulink, and bilateral cooperation programmes. Higher education, vocational education, sports, and training have developed into a combined format. On May 30, 2018, the European Commission adopted a proposal of over €26.2 billion to support mobility and cooperation in the period 2021-2027.

2. Bologna Process

Apart from the Erasmus programme, the EU supported the Bologna process for the internationalization of higher education and established various cooperative systems between the Erasmus programme and the Bologna process.[9]

In 1997, the Lisbon Recreation Convention was signed under the leadership of the Council of Europe, which included mutual recognition of university degrees and related certificates between European countries. In 1999, the ministers of education of 29 member countries of the Council of Europe adopted the Bologna Declaration, and the Bologna process was launched to rebuild a modernized higher education in Europe.

The purpose of the Bologna process is to remove barriers to higher education among European countries and establish a European Higher Education Area (EHEA) where an integrated system applies; as of 2021, 48 countries participate d in the Bologna process.[10]

In March 2000, the Lisbon European Council decided to link the higher education, represented by Erasmus Programme, with the Bologna process. The EU Member States share the EHEA goals set by the Bologna process and various projects and systems between the two sides.[11] The EU operates the European Credit Transfer and Accumulation System (ECTS) and the European Qualifications Framework (EQF) to compare and provide information on the degree system and academic level of Member States as a basic system for revitalizing student exchanges between higher educational institutions in Europe.

Meanwhile, the Bologna process added the Bologna Framework for Qualifications, more widely known as the Bologna cycle, and established the European Association for Quality Assessment (ENQA) for higher education institutions. [12] In addition, the EU ECTS is applied as it is, and the EQF and the Bologna cycle are mutually applied in the process of their programme.

Korea-EU Educational Cooperation

1. Korea-EU Cooperation Programmes

After Korea achieved rapid economic growth in the 1980s, Korea introduced the institutional development process of Korean higher education evaluation. At this time, capabilities and autonomy were very weak because they were in their early stages. However, since 1995, as the opening of higher education services began in earnest, the government-promoted internationalization of higher education in Korea.

Since 2000s, over the past 20 years, higher education institutions across Korea have developed internationalization policies to meet the needs of globalization of the 21st century. Korean universities have implemented internationalization policies through the provision of international graduate schools and enhanced student and professor exchange programmes.[13]

Following this policy Korea-EU educational cooperation increased, with a special push since 2011 when the Korea-EU Free Trade Agreement (FTA) was ratified. The EU's international political capabilities post-Lisbon Treaty function not only along with its status as a major global actor to allow significant influence in a wide range of world affairs but also brings to increase interest in the EU. In turn, the EU has focused on the Asia-Pacific region and especially Korea. The EU-Korea relationship gained traction given Korea's high economic profile and the strategic importance of Northeast Asia. Thus, there was increased interest in closer cooperation between the EU and Korea both in the realms of economics and socio-politics.

The ratification of the Korea-EU FTA and the renewed Framework Agreement between Korea and the EU in the early 2010s turn out to be the cornerstone of the envisioned Korea-EU strategic partnership. Based on this cooperation, on November 8, 2013, at the 7th Korea-EU summit, Korea and the EU agreed on a new era of cooperation in the field of education and strengthening higher education partnerships.[14] After the joint declaration, the educational cooperation between the two sides has become closer.

Based on this cooperative relationship, Korea and the EU share and implement educational cooperation programmes, like the ICI-ECP, Erasmus Mundus program, Jean Monet Activities, and the ASEM-DUO fellowship programme.

1.1) ICI-ECP

The EU started higher education cooperation projects with Japan and Australia as a pilot programme in 2002, and launched the ICI-ECP with expanding its target countries to Korea and New Zealand in 2008. The ICI-ECP programme was launched separately for educational cooperation with advanced industrial countries under the Erasmus Mundus programme,. The operation is juedged as successful regarding the equal academic level with the target country and the interest of students. However, the ICI-ECP between Korea and the EU suffered from the fact Korea did not have an institutional framework such as the ECTS. This hindered practical cooperation between Korea and the EU in various academic fields, and the ICI-ECP has been integrated into the Erasmus+ system since 2014.

1.2) Erasmus Mundus

The Erasmus Mundus I programme began with Master course in 2004, the Ph.D. course was added in 2009 through Erasmus Mundus II . Thanks to the master's course, about 2,000 students have been able to complete degree courses at higher education institutions in Europe annually since 2010. But competition has been very fierce as the door to Erasmsus is open to all countries around the world as well as the EU.[15] In the case of Korea, higher education through this programme was not conducted successfully because of the difficulty to compose well-matched consortium and high-level of competition with other countries' higher education institutions.

After 2014, the Erasmus Mundus program was integrated with the launch of the Erasmus+ system into the Erasmus Mundus Joint Degrees (EMJMD). Under the EMJMD, participating institutions should form a consortium between at least three higher educational institutions and all EU universities participating in the consortium must have different nationalities and at least one external country must participate. The Erasmus Plus program is an EU integrated funding system that supports education, training, youth, and sports, providing opportunities for students, trainees, youth, and volunteers, as well as professors, educational staff, and civic groups to gain educational and professional experience in other countries. Currently, more than 4 million students have been exempted from their subsidies and tuition fees, allowing them to study in other European countries.[16]

1.3) Jean Monnet Activities

Jean Monnet activities aim to promote European Studies and European Studies in the field of higher education. Specifically, they support education and research through Jean Monnet Modules, Jean Monnet

Chairs, and Jean Monnet Center of Excellence.[17] In addition, it provides policy discussions through Jean Monnet Networks and Jean Monnet Projects, and related research institutes and academic support. Currently in Korea, korean universities who operate the Jean Monnet Centres of Excellence are Hankuk University of Foreign Studies, Seoul National University, Yonsei University, and Korea University.

2. The Case of Hankuk University of Foreign Studies (HUFS)

Hankuk University of Foreign Studies (HUFS), as Korea's leading university in the domain of international and area studies, excels in the fields of both International Relations and EU Studies. HUFS already offers a very wide range of courses in these academic areas The Departments of International Studies and EU Studies at Graduate School of International Area Studies (GSIAS) plays a leading role. These Departments offer more than 30 courses in each academic term and the students are required to complete their MA or Ph.D. dissertations in order to fulfil their degree requirements.

At the undergraduate level, the university also runs the largest and most comprehensive programmes for International Relations (IR) and EU studies in Korea. While having an independent Faculty of International Studies, the university began to offer a joint BA degree programme in EU studies in 2005, enabling students to obtain two bachelor's degrees upon successful completion of the degree requirements. This programme has been continuously strengthened afterwards, by adopting a few new programmes. For instance, a BA/MA joint degree programme was introduced, allowing students to pursue the two degrees within five years, one year less than the standard case. Up to 100 undergraduates from HUFS are studying at European universities each year via various exchange programmes.

At the level of professors and researchers, IR and EU-related research has also been very active. The HUFS Institute of EU Studies has initiated numerous joint research projects with internationally recognized universities, research institutions and scholars/experts all around the world. In addition to organizing high-impact policy

Table 1. Major MOU and Cooperation with European Universities

No.	University	Country
1	Institut français des relations internationales	France
2	Vrije University Brussel	Belgium
3	College of Europe	
4	London School of Economics	United Kingdom
5	Henry Jackson Society	
6	Stockholm International Peace Research Institute	Sweden
7	University of Copenhagen	Denmark
8	Institut de Relations Internationales et Stratégiques	France
9	Real Instituto Elcano	Spain
10	Univerzita Karlova	Czech Republic
11	University of Bremen	Germany
12	Sofia University	Bulgaria
13	Eotvos Lorand University	Hungary
14	Vytautas Magnus University	Lithuania
15	University of Latvia	Latvia
16	Ss. Cyril and Methodius University in Skopje	Macedonia
17	Moldova State University	Moldova
18	Adam Mickiewicz University	Poland
19	University of Bucharest	Romania
20	University of Belgrade	Serbia
21	University of Ljubljana	Slovenia
22	University of Lviv	Ukraine

Source: Author Writing based on HUFS/GSIAS homepages.

workshops and international conferences with them, they have conducted a lot of joint research projects, which led to the production of numerous policy reports and proposals for the governments of Korea and other countries, as well as the publication of scholarly books and articles in Korea and abroad.

HUFS has established a world-wide web of networks with top-class universities, think tanks and research institutes of highest academic reputation. In the last decades, HUFS has been cradle of EU studies and entertained various exchange and joint/double degree programmes with a selected number of universities and research institutions in Europe. In addition, the University has established a solid foundation for research and education cooperation with a wide range of universities and institutions all around the world. HUFS carries out annual student and researcher exchanges and organises annual international seminars and conferences with these institutions. The following lists include a part of collaborating universities and institutions with which HUFS signed bilateral and multilateral MOUs and agreements.

2.1) ICI-ECP (2011-2014)

HUFS ICI-ECP was a joint mobility project that carried out a Korea-EU student exchange project to institutionalize Korea-EU partnership for three years. Participating universities were four universities in Europe, which are Institut d'Etudes Politiques de Bordeaux (France), Universitat Autonoma de Barcelona (Spain), Vrije Universiteit Brussel (Belgium) and Ca' Foscari University of Venice (Italy). HUFS had selected 4-5 outstanding graduate students in the GSIAS each semester to give them the opportunity to study abroad and to become regional experts with expertise and practical skills to play a key role in various areas of Korea-EU partnership, including economy, trade, diplomacy, and culture. This program also improves the quality of higher education, vocational training and the understanding of other cultures. It includes financial support to students from advanced industrial countries and exchange and cooperation with European students.

2.2) HUFS-HRI EU Centre (2011-2015)

HUFS-HRI EU Centre was established in 2011 cooperating with Hyundai Research Institute (HRI). The Centre carried out a wide range of activities related to EU policy, as well as programs to educate students in studing European integration. The EU Centre was an educational, research and external activity organization established by the European Commission in the Asia-Pacific region to raise awareness of the European Union and promote education and research related to the European Union. Since the first EU Centre was established in the United States and Canada in 1998, over 26 centres have been established in the United States, Canada, Australia, New Zealand, Japan, Korea, Singapore, and Taiwan.

HUFS-HRI EU Centre was pursuing four main goals were as follows:[18]

- Conducting educational programmes on various topics on European integration shall be established and research activities
- Integrated European education and research by establishing a network between domestic and foreign EU centres
- Improving the understanding of EU and community policy in Korea through various external activities.

Table 2. Main Programmes of HUFS-HRI EU Centre

No.	Category	Activities
1	Academic Research	EU Young Challenge Publications of Report and Books National/International Conference Curriculum Development of EU Major
2	Education	Meet the EU Lecture Future Expert Training Programme. Experts and Entrepreneurs Forum EU Certificate Course
3	Cooperation and Promotion	Broadcasting and Video Programme EU Barometer Survey EU Centres Networking Digital Service (Homepage, Applications and etc)

Source: Author Writing.

2.3) Jean Monnet Lifelong Learning Programme (2012-2013)

HUFS Jean Monnet Lifelong Learning Programme, a part of the EU Jean Monnet Programme, was to inspire awareness of the European Union under the theme of "EU Learning in Korea." HUFS Jean Monnet Lifelong Learning Programme hosted events for Korean middle and high school students to raise awareness of the European Union and expand cultural exchanges. The selection of the program can be seen as the result of the European Union's recognition of the capabilities and achievements of the HUFS in relation to European Union studies. It is also very significant that HUFS was the only one selected in Asia.

2.4) HUFS Jean Monnet Centre of Excellence (2016-2021)

HUFS Jean Monnet Centre of Excellence was established to promote excellence in teaching and research in the field of European Union studies in Korea. The actions taken by the Centre are focused at fostering the dialogue between the academic world and policymakers, with the aim of raising awareness about governance of EU policies., HUFS Jean Monnet Centre has dealt with three areas of connectivity: security, economy and trade, and mobility. Throughout these activities, the Centre gathers the expertise both at home and abroad of high level of competence. Academic, professional and governmental agencies are invited to provide added value and simultaneously to create 1.5 Track diplomacy. Thereby the Centre contributes not only to policy making but even law-making . In terms of academic endeavours, the HUFS Jean Monnet Centre created a Centre of academic excellence in EU studies by strengthening the EU knowledge base among students, teaching staff and researchers. The project also introduced new EU-related courses in various departments and a graduate school of international and area studies(GSIAS).

Table 3. Academic and Research Goals of HUFS Jean Monnet EU Centre

State	Subject	Contents
1st Stage (2016-19)	EU-related interdisciplinary Research	Politics: Foreign, Security, and Defense Policy for the EU-East Asian Cooperation Economy: The EU Northeast Asian Relations regarding Trade and Legal System Ideology: Ideology of European Integration and its Application to Northeast Asia
2nd Stage (2019-21)	Korea-EU Connectivity Research	Security Connectivity between Europe and Asia Economic and Trade Connectivity between Europe and Asia Social/Cultural Connectivity between Europe and Asia

Source: Author Writing.

Conclusion

Korea has developed rapidly amid the trend of globalization, and has achieved the status of a middle power country that can create values and norms in the international community. Korea is emerging as a leading player in public diplomacy in the international community based on culture and digital diplomacy. In line with these capabilities and under the COVID-19 pandemic, the importance of non-contact education using digital technology and online platform in the field of educational cooperation is growing[19] Accordingly, in order to keep up with the expectations of international community, Korea needs to strengthen cooperation with other countries along with the internationalization of Korean education by utilizing digital capability.

In particular, considering the size of the trade volume, the quality level of higher education institutions, and the proportion of R&D expenditures to GDP between the two sides, educational cooperation with Europe is much more important than with any other region. Therefore, Korea-EU cooperation in the field of higher education needs to be further strengthened. However, several factors which constrain educational cooperation between Korea and the EU need to be overcome: First, both Korea and the EU are actively promoting the internationalization of higher education, but Korea is focusing on attracting Asian students, including China. On the other hand, the EU focuses primarily on exchanges between Member States and f on exchanges with non-EU countries through the Bologna process. In addition, the EU promotes the exchange programme in higher education, focusing on the third world, which has deep political and economic relations with Europe. Second, the EU has established various higher education certification and support systems since the 1990s, including the ECTS. In addition, through cooperation with the Bologna process, the EU has integrated systems for higher education management such as credit certification, degree, and qualitative certification through EHEA. On the other hand, Korea does not yet set a practical system for mobility and exchange programmes with higher education institutions around the world.

Therefore, in order to promote educational cooperation between Korea and the EU more effectively, a more systematic cooperation system and programmes should be created through continuous dialogue and discussion on the issue. The top priority for this is to establish a system corresponding to the credit certification and qualitative certification systems commonly used in Europe.Considering that European higher education system is dualized into the EU Erasmus programme and the Bologna process, Korea needs to pursue a bilateral approach of educational cooperation with the EU, its Member States, and non-EU countries.

---

1 Maria da Conceição Pereira Ramos (2014), "Mobility, Internationalisation, Higher Education: European Challenges," Alina Mihaela Dima *et al.* (eds.), *Handbook of Research on Trends in European Higher Education Convergence*, IGI Global.

2 Barragán Codina, José Nicolás & Leal López, and Rubén Hernán (2013), "The Importance of Student Mobility, Academic Exchange and Internationalization of Higher Education for College Students in a Globalized World: The Mexican and Latin American Case," *International Journal of Good Conscience*, Vol. 8, No. 2, http://www.spentamexico.org/v8-n2/A3.8(2)48-63.pdf

3 International Organization for Migration(IOM) (2019), WORLD MIGRATION REPORT 2020, https://publications.iom.int/system/files/pdf/wmr_2020.pdf

4 Council of the European Union (1987), 87/327/EEC: Council Decision of 15 June 1987 adopting the European Community Action Scheme for the Mobility of University Students (Erasmus)

5 European Commission (2017), From Erasmus to Erasmus+: a story of 30 years, https://ec.europa.eu/commission/presscorner/detail/en/MEMO_17_83

6 European Commission (2021), Erasmus+ Programme Guide, Eligible countries. https://erasmus-plus.ec.europa.eu/programme-guide/erasmusplus-programme-guide

7 loyd, Christine (2013), "The Erasmus Mundus programme: providing opportunities to develop a better understanding about inclusion and inclusive practice through an international collaborative programme of study," *International Journal of Inclusive Education*. Vol. 17, No. 4 pp. 329–335.

8 Ibid., p. 334.

9 European Commission (2014), Erasmus+ The EU programme for Education, Training, Youth and Sport 2014-2020, https://erasmus-plus.ec.europa.eu/

10 John McCormick (2011), Understanding the European Union, 5th. ed., Palgrave Macmillan, p. 389.

11 Åse Gornitzka (2006), "The Open Method of Coordination as Practice - A Watershed in European Education Policy?" Advanced Research on the Europeanisation of the Nation-State, Working Papers 06/16, p. 15.

12 ENQA (2016), European Association for Quality Assurance in Higher Education, History. https://www.enqa.eu/

13 John D. Palmer, Young Ha Cho (2012), "South Korean higher education internationalization policies: perceptions and experiences," *Asia Pacific Education Review*, Vol. 13, pp. 387–401

14 European Commission (2013), Higher Education: EU and Korea agree new era of cooperation, https://ec.europa.eu/commission/presscorner/detail/en/IP_13_1061

15 European Commission (2016), Erasmus Mundus joint master's degrees: the story so far, p. 7. https://op.europa.eu/en/publication-detail/-/publication/6f52e9bb-31f2-11e6-b497-01aa75ed71a1

16 Sue Hubble, Alex Bellis, Paul Bolton (2021), "The Erasmus Programme", p. 4. https://researchbriefings.files.parliament.uk/documents/CBP-8326/CBP-8326.pdf.

17 European Commission, Jean Monnet Actions: stimulating teaching and research on the European Union, https://erasmus-plus.ec.europa.eu/opportunities/organisations/jean-monnet-actions-stimulating-teaching-and-research-on-the-european-union

18 HUFS-HRI EU Centre, https://www.hufs.ac.kr/user/hrieng/

19 Kim Ho, Kim Yong Hee (2021), "Non-contact Education in ASEAN and the Proposal of ASEAN Educational Development Cooperation after COVID-19," *Southeast Asia Journal*, Vol. 31, pp. 300-301.

Bibliography

Åse Gornitzka (2006). "The Open Method of Coordination as Practice - A Watershed in European Education Policy?" *Advanced Research on the Europeanisation of the Nation-State*. Working Papers 06/16.

Barragán Codina, José Nicolás & Leal López, and Rubén Hernán (2013). "The Importance of Student Mobility, Academic Exchange and Internationalization of Higher Education for College Students in a Globalized World: The Mexican and Latin American Case." *International Journal of Good Conscience*. Vol. 8 No. 2. http://www.spentamexico.org/v8-n2/A3.8(2)48-63.pdf

Council of the European Union (1987). 87/327/EEC: Council Decision of 15 June 1987 adopting the European Community Action Scheme for the Mobility of University Students (Erasmus)

ENQA (2016). European Association for Quality Assurance in Higher Education, History. https://www.enqa.eu/

European Commission (2013). Higher Education: EU and Korea agree new era of cooperation. https://ec.europa.eu/commission/presscorner/detail/en/IP_13_1061

________ (2014). Erasmus+ The EU programme for Education, Training, Youth and Sport 2014-2020. https://erasmus-plus.ec.europa.eu/

________ (2016). Erasmus Mundus joint master degrees The story so far. https://op.europa.eu/en/publication-detail/-/publication/6f52e9bb-31f2-11e6-b497-01aa75ed71a1

________ (2017). From Erasmus to Erasmus+: a story of 30 years, https://ec.europa.eu/commission/presscorner/detail/en/MEMO_17_83

________ (2021). Erasmus+ Programme Guide, Eligible countries.
https://erasmus-plus.ec.europa.eu/programme-guide/erasmusplus-programme-guide

________ (2021). Jean Monnet Actions: stimulating teaching and research on the European Union, https://erasmus-plus.ec.europa.eu/opportunities/organisations/jean-monnet-actions-stimulating-teaching-and-research-on-the-european-union

HUFS GSIAS, http://gsias.hufs.ac.kr/

HUFS Jean Monnet Centre, http://www.hufs.ac.kr/user/hri/

HUFS-HRI EU Centre, https://www.hufs.ac.kr/user/hrieng/

International Organization for Migration(IOM) (2019). WORLD MIGRATION REPORT 2020 https://publications.iom.int/system/files/pdf/wmr_2020.pdf

John D. Palmer, Cho Young Ha (2012). "South Korean higher education internationalization policies: perceptions and experiences." *Asia Pacific Education Review*. Vol. 13.

John McCormick (2011). Understanding the European Union, 5th. ed., Palgrave Macmillan.

Christine Loyd (2013). "The Erasmus Mundus programme: providing opportunities to develop a better understanding about inclusion and inclusive practice through an international collaborative programme of study." *International Journal of Inclusive Education*. Vol. 17 No. 4.

Kim Bong Chul, Shin Eui Chan (2021). "Institutions and Activities of Research and Education of European Studies in Korean Universities." *The Journal of Contemporary European Studies*. Vol. 39 No. 4.

Kim Ho, Kim Yong Hee (2021). "Non-contact Education in ASEAN and the Proposal of ASEAN Educational Development Cooperation after COVID-19." *Southeast Asia Journal*. Vol. 31.

Maria da Conceição Pereira Ramos (2014). "Mobility, Internationalisation, Higher Education: European Challenges." Alina Mihaela Dima *et al.* (eds.). *Handbook of Research on Trends in European Higher Education Convergence*. IGI Global.

Connecting Europe and Korea
Cooperation in Science Research and Innovation

Tomasz Wierzbowski

Towards EU
Korea collaboration in Science Research and Innovation (SR&I)

Korea[1] is one of the eleven EU's strategic partners, with bonds built on agreements covering economic, political, and security cooperation, as well as collaboration in areas of science, technology and innovation. The EU-Korea Strategic Partnership is underpinned by three concrete pillars: an enhanced Partnership and Cooperation Agreement; an ambitious Free Trade Agreement; and a Framework Participation Agreement for EU crisis management operations.

Being aware that Science, Technology, and Innovation play a crucial role in shaping the world economy, the EU and Korea signed the Agreement on the Scientific and Technological Cooperation in 2007. This was preceded by the Agreement for Cooperation between Euratom and Korea in the field of fusion energy research in force since 2006; its EU-Korea Joint Science & Technology Cooperation Committee (JSTCC) has been held biennially. The 7th JSTCC scheduled for spring 2020 fell victim to the COVID-19 pandemic and finally took place in Seoul on 14 February 2022 under the co-chairmanship of Director-General of the Directorate General for Research and Innovation of the European Commission, Mr. Jean-Eric Paquet, and Vice Minister of

Science and ICT of Korea, Mr. Yong Hongtaek. The meeting, conducted in hybrid mode was attended by high level Korean officials from MSIT, Korean Research Centres, Science Counsellors from Member States and EU officials. As a result of the JSTCC both sides defined five priority areas for cooperation: Information and Communication Technology (ICT); Health/Bio; Climate Change, Emerging Future Technology; Research Hub and Human capital development.

In order to intensify cooperation, EURAXESS - Researchers in Motion, initiative was launched in May 2018. EURAXESS is a European Commission initiative delivering information and support services to professional researchers. Backed by the EU, Member States and associated countries, this program supports researcher mobility and career development, while enhancing scientific collaboration between Europe and Korea.

EU Science and Research Policy

With only 7% of the world's population, Europe accounts for 20% of global R&D investment, produces one third of all high-quality scientific publications, and holds a world leading position in industrial sectors such as pharmaceuticals, chemicals, mechanical engineering, and fashion. Furthermore, research and innovation have been key to battling the ongoing coronavirus pandemic.

Since 1984, The EU's research and technological development activities have been defined and implemented by a series of Framework Programmes for Research and Technological Development (Framework Programmes, FP, or FP1-FP9).

The FPs have been the main financial tools through which the EU supports research and development activities covering almost all scientific disciplines. FPs are proposed by the European Commission and adopted by the member states in the Council and the European Parliament. The budget for FPs started with 3.8 billion Euro for FP1 and has increased ever since to Euro 95.5 billion for the present for Horizon Europe (FP9).[2]

Horizon Europe

Horizon Europe or FP9, focuses on improving the objectives in the previous framework, Horizon 2020, by supporting a broad range of member state science and research projects.

While the implementation was delayed by COVID-19, a political agreement was reached in November 2020 between the European Parliament, EU Member States in the Council, the Commission on the next long-term EU budget, and NextGenerationEU. 95.5 billion Euro were earmarked for Horizon Europe, including 5.4 billion Euro from Next GenerationEU to foster recovery from the COVID-19 pandemic and additional reinforcement of 4.5 billion Euro.

Horizon Europe Structure

The complex funding structure of Horizon Europe follows previous Framework Programmes and rests on three pillars: Excellent Science; Global Challenges and European Industrial Competitiveness; and Innovative Europe.

The first pillar

The Excellent Science pillar is directed to researchers through fellowships, exchanges, and funding projects defined and driven by researchers themselves. The pillar consists of the European Research Council, Marie-Skłodowska-Curie Actions, and Research Infrastructures programs.

The European Research Council (ERC) aims to support the best and the most creative researchers to identify and explore new opportunities and directions in any field of science: physical sciences, engineering, life science, social sciences, and humanities. The ERC does not prioritize any area of research and is investigator-driven e.g., a bottom-up approach researchers themselves propose projects. Projects crossing disciplinary boundaries, addressing new and emerging fields and introducing unconventional and innovative approaches to stimulate scientific

Figure 1: Structure of Horizon Europe

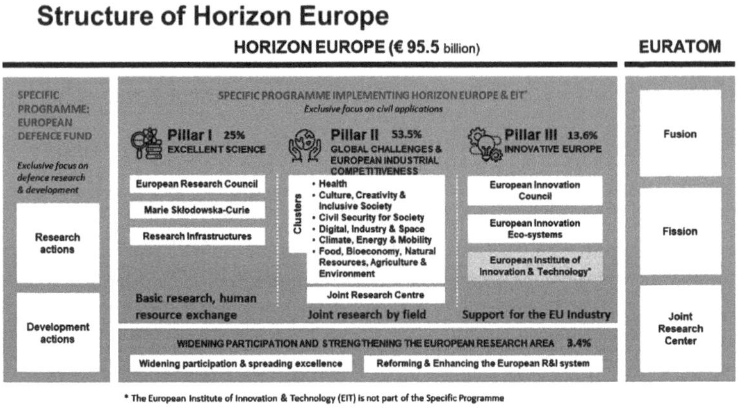

excellence across Europe, are specifically encouraged. The ERC awards long-term grants to individual researchers of any nationality and age from anywhere in the world who intend to carry out their research projects in a host organization based in Europe (European Research Area). Excellence is the sole evaluation criterion. Under Horizon Europe, the ERC has a total budget over 16 billion Euro for the period 2021 – 2027.[3]

Marie Skłodowska-Curie Actions (MSCA) is a research fellowship program that supports researchers at all stages of their careers from all over the world regardless of age. Researchers from all scientific fields from engineering and mathematics to life science, social sciences and humanities can benefit from the program. Furthermore, the MSCA scheme supports not only individual researchers, who can apply with their own original ideas through a bottom-up approach, but the program also enhances cooperation between industry and academia. It provides innovative training for academic staff with the aim to strengthen employability and career development. The MSCA are open to all domains of research and innovation, from fundamental research to market take-up and innovation services. The program addresses the challenges faced by researchers, offering them attractive working conditions and the opportunity to move between academic and other settings. Under Horizon 2020 the MSCA budget was 6.2 billion Euro, which is 8% of the total budget. For Horizon Europe the budget will be increased by 6.4% to 6.6 billion Euro in funding.[4]

Research Infrastructures (RI) address how communities will contribute to the five mission areas of Horizon Europe. The work of the European Strategy Forum on Research Infrastructures (ESFRI) resulted in the development of plans for 55 European RI, of which 37 have already been implemented across all fields of science, mobilizing close to 20 billion Euro in investments[5]. Between 2014-2020, funding new world-class research infrastructures had a 2.48 billion Euro budget, and a 2.4 billion Euro budget is estimated under Horizon Europe.[6]

The second pillar

The second Pillar under Horizon Europe–Global Challenges & Industrial Competitiveness–enables and promotes research that explicitly address the most pressing societal issues clustered in six thematic areas (top-down approach):

1. Health: aimed to better understand and manage health and diseases, including cross-border health risks and infections, to deliver integrated, people-centered, equal health and care across Europe, and a sustainable digital transformation of European healthcare systems with cross-border secure and ethical data management;
2. Culture, Creativity and Inclusive Societies: expected to enhance research focused on democratic governance and citizen participation, culture heritage and creativity;
3. Civil Security for Society: boosting research on how to provide security for citizens through police, civil protection, customs, law enforcement agencies, and the policies that govern them as well as targeting research on cybersecurity and data protection;
4. Digital, Industry, and Space: aimed to promote the transition to a climate-neutral, circular, and environmentally friendly industry, and enable research on clean, safe and accessible transport and mobility;

5. Climate, Energy, and Mobility: will promote research on clean energy supply and storage, smart clean and safe transportation, solutions on greenhouse gas emissions, and alignment with the European Green Deal to achieve climate neutrality by 2050;
6. Food, Bioeconomy, Natural Resources, Agriculture, and the Environment: enables research aimed to decrease the negative impact of food production and agriculture on environment, to stop the depletion of biodiversity reconstruction of ecosystems, as well as researched focused on resources management and food and water safety.[7]

The societal issues tackled by the six thematic areas are often complex and require interdisciplinary approaches. In this context social sciences and humanities play a significant role and should be included in the research approach.

The second pillar also aims to improve Europe's competitiveness in technologies covered by the six thematic areas. Call for proposals are systematically open during the duration of Horizon Europe.

Part of this pillar, the Joint Research Centre, provides EU policy makers independent scientific evidence and technical support. Through the European Atomic Energy Community's research and training program, the Joint Research Center also supports the EU's efforts to strengthen nuclear safety, citizens' safety, and radiation protection.

Approximately 48 billion Euro (52.7%) of the total Horizon Europe budget is allocated to cover research under the second pillar with cluster 4 (Digital, Industry and Space) and cluster 5 (Climate, Energy and Mobility) having secured the largest part of the budget of 13.4 billion Euro.

The third pillar

Programs previously covered by the third pillar of Horizon 2020 (Societal Challenges) were incorporated into the second pillar of Horizon Europe and a new pillar was conceptualized - Innovative Europe. This pillar aims to make Europe a leader in market-creating innovation. A new funding body, the European Innovation Council (EIC) was introduced in order to support high-risk, high-impact ideas that would turn scientific achievements into new businesses and increase the size and number of so called "game-changing" innovators. The impetus for creating the European Innovation councils was the number of start-ups. The EU is among world leaders in research into artificial intelligence but lags far behind other regions in bringing it to market. The EU is home to only 8% of €1 billion start-ups ("unicorns"), far below the US (home to almost 50% of the world's unicorns) and Asia. The goal of the European Innovation Council (EIC) is to put Europe on top of the next wave of breakthrough and disruptive innovation that creates new markets, in particular by combining physical and digital products and services based on new technologies business models. It aims to make Europe an internationally attractive place to develop, invest, and scale up highly innovative technologies and companies. The EIC is open for ideas in any field of innovation. Applications are possible any time. The EIC has two types of innovators in mind: (i) Pathfinder – a researcher with an innovative idea for the next breakthrough technology; and (ii) Accelerator – a start-up, SME or entrepreneur with a business plan to develop and scale up a high-risk (but high-gain) enterprise.[8]

The pillar also includes the activities of the European Innovation Ecosystems and the European Institute of Innovation and Technology.

The European Innovation Ecosystems (EIE) aims to connect ecosystems across Europe and provide the possibility to access complementary skills, infrastructure, and markets. Collaborating ecosystems can form alliances to confront and overcome various societal challenges. The EIE focuses on ecosystem building and strengthening as well as supporting collaboration between various ecosystems.[9]

The European Institute of Innovation and Technology (EIT) is an independent EU body based in Budapest that is strengthening Europe's ability to innovate. EIT promotes and strengths synergies and cooperation between businesses, education institutions, and research organizations to form dynamic cross-border partnerships. EIT empowers innovators and entrepreneurs to turn their best ideas into products, services, jobs, and growth.[10]

The Innovative Europe pillar has a total budget of 11.8 billion Euro.

The de facto fourth pillar

The underlying fourth component of Horizon Europe structure, Widening Participation and Strengthening the European Research Area (ERA), provides support to the EU Member States to increase their national research and innovation capacities. A special focus is put on encouraging countries that perform lower in research and innovation.

The ERA was launched in 2020 in the context of the Lisbon Strategy to address the fragmentation of the EU's research and innovation system, which at the time consisted of the juxtaposition of the national R&I systems and an EU level funding program. ERA aims to build a common scientific and technological area for the EU and create a single market for research and innovation fostering free movement of researchers, scientific knowledge, and innovation, and encouraging a more competitive European industry. This involves restructuring the European research landscape toward more cross-border cooperation, continent-wide competition, building of critical mass and coordination, and the improvement of national research policies and systems.

Over the last 20 years significant progress has been made in removing the geographical barriers to researchers' mobility and the fragmentation of research careers in Europe, driven by the European Charter for Researchers and a Code of Conduct[11] for the Recruitment of Researchers already adopted by 1,242 organizations. In addition, the EURAXESS[12] initiative supports researcher mobility and career development by delivering information and support services to professional researchers.

The ERA has enhanced access to open, free of charge, re-usable scientific information through the Open Science initiative[13] and the recently launched European Open Science Cloud (EOSC) which created a cloud area for research data in Europe allowing for better science through open and collaborative knowledge sharing.

The Horizon Europe Strategy

The European Commission emphasizes the importance of strategic planning to remain flexible, and to be able to respond promptly to unexpected crisis, such as the COVID-19 pandemic. The Horizon Europe implementation strategy focuses on maximizing impacts; ensuring greater transparency and further simplification; fostering synergies with other EU spending programs; and easing access through digital transformation and outreach.

The strategic planning process focuses in particular on the second pillar of Horizon Europe 'Global challenges and European industrial competitiveness'. It also covers relevant activities in the first pillar, 'Excellent Science', and the third pillar, 'Innovative Europe', and the 'Widening Participation and Strengthening the European Research Area part'. This first Horizon Europe strategic plan defines the strategic orientations for our research and innovation investments over the period 2021-2024 and acts as a compass to stay on course with the political priorities of the Commission with a focus on a climate neutral and green Europe, fit for the digital age, where the economy works for the people. The aim is to ensure an effective interface between EU policy priorities, and programme activities and ultimately, the research and innovation projects funded by Horizon Europe. This will stimulate research and innovation investments where they are needed and, most importantly, deliver results. Horizon Europe will approach the twin transitions towards a green and digital recovery in an ambitious manner and will commit sizeable financial efforts to support the green and digital transformations. In order to reflect the need to accelerate these transitions following the COVID-19 pandemic, the degree of investment will be considerably increased compared to the current programming period and proportionate to the level of ambition of the Commission within these areas. The EU Member States, European Economic Area (EEA) Countries and the European Parliament, as well as stakeholders and interested citizens, all made a collective effort to design it.[14]

Missions under Horizon Europe

A new component under this Framework Programme is called "Missions", A Mission area is defined as a portfolio of actions intended to achieve a bold, inspirational, and measurable goal within a set timeframe that will impact science, technology, society, and citizens beyond individual actions.[15] The missions relevant to a broad range of stakeholders and to citizens should be completed using a bottom-up approach.

There are five mission areas aimed to address some of the world's biggest challenges. Each mission has a dedicated mission board and assembly. The board and assembly help specify, design, and implement the specific missions which will launch under Horizon Europe in 2021. The five missions will address five societal challenges as discussed below.

Figure 2: Horizon Europe Missions

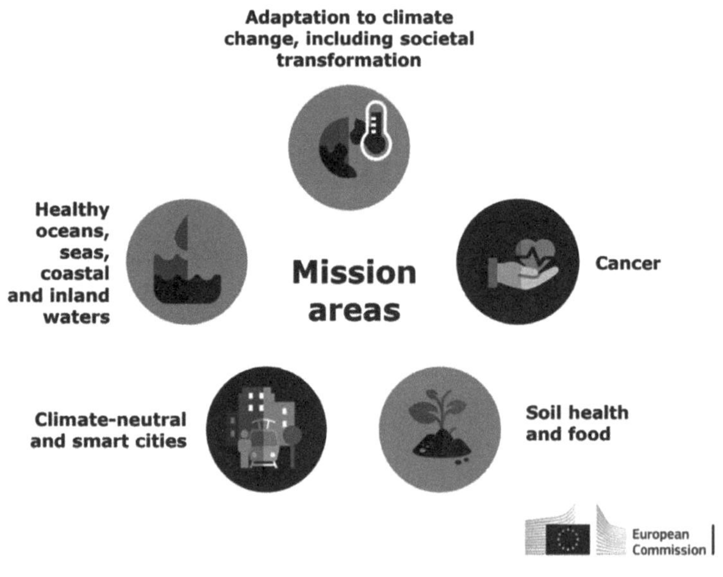

Source: EU Commission

Adaptation to climate change, including societal transformation

This mission copes with the rapidly heating earth. The COVID-19 crisis underlined the importance of being prepared for unexpected situations. This mission will focus on solutions and preparedness for the impact of climate change to protect lives and assets. It will include behavioral changes and social aspects by addressing new communities beyond the usual stakeholders, which will help lead to a societal transformation. The mission will tackle the climate threat as an opportunity to improve social resilience and standard of living.[16]

By 2030, this mission is supposed to: prepare Europe to deal with climate disruptions, and assist all citizens, communities and regions in better understanding, preparing for, and managing climate risks; accelerate the transformation to a climate-resilient future, supporting 200 European communities and regions in co-creating a vision, innovation pathways, and developing solutions for transformative adaptation within safe planetary boundaries; and build deep resilience by scaling up actionable solutions triggering societal transformations through 100 deep demonstrations of resilience across a number of European communities and regions, with emphasis on cross-border cooperation and cohesion.

Cancer

The Mission related to cancer will address the entire cancer control continuum from prevention of risk factors to survivorship support and end-of-life care for all ages and cancers, including: rare and poorly understood cancers, cancers in children, adolescents/young adults and the elderly, cancers in socially or economically vulnerable families and among people living in remote areas, across all Member States. While the Mission provides directions and objectives for research and innovation, it will also generate evidence on factors that limit effective policy and support actions to conquer cancer. In this regard, this Mission's actions will be able to make an important contribution to Europe's Beating Cancer Plan and this Cancer Plan will provide opportunities to complement the Mission on Cancer.[17]

By 2030, this Mission should save more than 3 million lives in addition to helping patients live longer and better, achieving a thorough understanding of cancer, preventing what is preventable, optimizing diagnosis and treatment, supporting the quality of life of all people exposed to cancer, and ensuring equitable access to the above across Europe.[18]

Soil health and food

The Mission's goal is to "ensure that 75% of soils are healthy by 2030 and are able to provide essential ecosystem services" such as the provision of food and other biomass, supporting biodiversity, storing and regulating the flow of water, and mitigating the effects of climate change. The target corresponds to a 100% increase of healthy soils against the current baseline. This interim report sets out the vision and the blueprint to reach this ambition through a combination of research and innovation, training, and advice, as well as the demonstration of good practices for soil management using "Living labs" (experiments and innovation in a laboratory on the ground) and "Lighthouses" (places to showcase good practices).

Living Labs are defined as user-centred, open innovation ecosystems based on a systematic user co-creation approach integrating research and innovation processes in real life communities and settings. In practice, Living Labs place the citizen at the center of innovation, and have thus shown the ability to better mold the opportunities offered by new ICT concepts and solutions to the specific needs and aspirations of local contexts, cultures, and creativity potentials.

The Helsinki Manifesto (November 2006 Finnish EU Presidency[19]) first pointed at Living Labs as a first step towards "a new European R&D and Innovation System, entailing a major paradigm shift for the whole innovation process".[20]

Lighthouses are single sites, like a farm or a park, where to showcase good practices. These are places for demonstration and peer-to-peer learning. Here good practices are tested or in place and can be showed to inspire other practitioners to move towards sustainable land management. In addition, in lighthouse sites, researchers work together with land managers to ensure that research responds to concrete needs encountered in the field.[21]

To be successful, the mission will also improve the monitoring of soil health and the pressures acting on them, mobilize investments, and encourage changes in policies. The mission will be a joint endeavor by stakeholders, researchers, policy-makers, and citizens alike that will put Europe on a path toward sustainable land and soil management as part of a wider, green societal transition.[22]

Climate-neutral and smart cities

The Mission supports, promotes and showcases 100 European cities in their systemic transformation toward climate neutrality by 2030 and will make these cities into experimentation and innovation hubs for all cities. Cities are the place where decarbonization strategies for energy, transport, buildings and even industry and agriculture coexist and intersect. The climate emergency must be tackled within cities and by engaging citizens who are not only political actors in a governance structure, but also users, producers, consumers, and owners. Through a multi-level and co-creative process formalized in a Climate City Contract, adjusted to the realities of each city, the Mission is fully anchored in the European Green Deal Strategy to make Europe climate neutral by 2050.[23]

Healthy oceans, seas, coastal and inland waters

This Mission aims to regenerate our European ocean and waters by 2030, by reducing human pressures on marine and freshwater environments, restoring degraded ecosystems and sustainably harnessing the essential goods and services they provide. Protecting and restoring our ocean and waters is one of the defining tasks of our time, as human existence and all life on this planet fundamentally depend on them. The ocean and waters hold solutions to feed, power and heal our citizens. Yet for too long, societies have ignored their existential and environmental role and have not given them the attention they require, which risks turning ocean and waters from source of life to a threat to our way of life.[24]

Korea and Framework Programmes

Key Figures[25]

489 applications from Korea were submitted under the Horizon 2020 program which constituted 2,05% of all the proposals received worldwide. Of these applications 385 were eligible proposals[26] (2,62% of the total number of proposals). As a result, 115 organizations got successfully involved in H2020 projects which makes 0,07% of the total of number participants. Those organizations signed 83 grant agreements[27] which amounted to the total net EU contribution of 2,44 million Euro. This corresponds to 1,17% of total net EU contributions[28] to other countries.

In Korea, 61,9 % of all applications were submitted by research performing organizations, 20,2% by higher or secondary education institutions, 15% by public bodies (excl. research and education), 2,9 % came from the private sector. The top organization was the International Vaccine Institute with 1,42-million-euro net EU contribution, followed by Seoul National University (492,550 euro), and the Korea Technology Finance Corporation (208,130 euro). Regarding participation[29], the Korea Advanced Institute of Science and Technology with 9 projects was at the top of the list, followed by the Electronics and Telecommunications Research Institute (7), and the Korea Institute of Science and Technology (6) at the third place.

25 Korean organizations or individuals were involved in Horizon 2020 projects financed under Marie Skłodowska-Curie Actions which represented 0,96% of other countries total. Out of those 25 organizations, 21 were MSCA unique participants[30] which constituted 2,56% of other countries total. Two Korean legal entities were granted funding within a framework of the European Innovation Council (EIC) scheme, and that comprised 8% of all the other countries total. 15 experts were involved in the H2020 evaluation process, out of which 46,67% were female experts. 37,67% Korean proposals were evaluated per expert which is a visibly higher number comparing with other countries' average – 32,65%.

There were no ERC Principal Investigator chosen among Korean applicants, no Korean proposal was awarded the Seal of Excellence[31].

Participation in Programs

Korea ranked 9th out of 24 other countries which got exceptional funding with 2,44-million-euro total contribution for Korea. (Out of those 24 other countries The United States received unprecedented funding of 128,25 million euro.)

30 Korean research performing organizations were funded with research grants under H2020 pillar one – Excellent Science, including 25 under MSCA and 5 under Research Infrastructure. 82 Korean participations were included in a project funded under Pillar 2 – Global Challenges and European Industrial Competitiveness, including mainly 17 in the thematic field of information and communication technologies; 12 in the field of advanced materials; 11 in the area of secure, clean and efficient energy; 8 regarding climate action, environment, resource efficiency, and raw materials, etc. 2 Korean legal entities were granted funding under H2020 pillar 3 – Innovative Europe, within a framework

of European Innovation Council (EIC) scheme.

The Korean participation across Framework Programs increased from 67 in FP7 to 115 in H2020, while EU contribution across programs significantly rose from 1,94 million under FP 7 to 2,44 million euro under the Horizon 2020.

Collaboration with other countries

Korea's top European collaborators in H2020 are Germany (270 collaboration links[32]), the United Kingdom (239 collaboration links), Spain (237 collaboration links), and France (230 collaboration links). Korean institutions participated in the number of grand-scale H2020 undertakings, including *Internet of Food and Farm 2020*[33] with a net EU contribution of 29,999 million euro; *5G cooperative & connected automated MOBIlity on X-border corridors*[34] with a net EU contribution of 21,410 million euro; *AUTOmated driving Progressed by Internet Of Things*[35] with a net EU contribution of 19,924 million euro – all three projects were funded under Industrial Leadership pillar II, Information and Communication Technologies thematic priority. In the field of Societal Challenges, Korea participated in projects such as *Advancing novel and promising TB vaccine candidates for discovery to preclinical and early clinical development*[36] with a net EU contribution of 18,200 million euro, and *Integrated Arctic observation system*[37] with a net EU contribution of 15,490 million euro.

10 SMEs from Korea submitted their applications[38] which constituted 2,04% of country total involvement, and 7 Korean SMEs were involved in H2020 projects which constituted 6,09% of Koreas total participation. Additionally, 2 Korean SMEs were granted funding under the European Innovation Council.

Beyond the Horizon

Another initiative created to advance and promote the cooperation between the EU and non-EU countries such as Korea in the field of science and technology is the EU Partnership Instrument (PI). As a direct result of the collaboration between the EU Delegation to Korea and its public authorities, companies, civil society organizations, universities and individuals, a number of PI projects have emerged in the country. The key PI projects covers topics such as environment and green economy (The EU Gateway Program); climate change (Implementation of an Emissions Trading System in Korea); trade facilitation (Implementation of ILO Fundamental Convention 111 in Korea and the EU Member States). Other ongoing PI - EU-RoK Policy Dialogue Support Facility is aimed to strengthen the EU – Korea Strategic partnership by providing decision makers relevant information and expertise from experts in various fields.

Korean organizations participating in international R&D projects are also eligible for funding through EUREKA Network projects, Globalstars, Eurostars and Clusters programs. Eureka was established in 1985 as an agreement between 18 countries and the European Commission to foster competitiveness and market integration and to encourage R&D cooperation. Since then, EUREKA has expanded to include 48 countries (in Europe and beyond) who share the same goals and provide national funding to organizations who apply through our programs.

Over the years, programs like Eureka have been tailored to best support international industry-led R&D. These offer flexibility for international partners (Network projects and Globalstars), encourage mixed consortia with large companies (Clusters), allow SMEs to aim higher (Eurostars), support research and business ventures in new markets (Innowwide) and drive companies towards private investment (investment readiness).[39]

What is ahead?

Since 2018 connectivity has become a cornerstone of the EU's Indo-Pacific Strategy. Connectivity is a multi-layered concept but for the EU 'connectivity' is primarily about the networks that bring people, places and opportunities closer together, with a particular focus on transport, energy, digital and human-to-human connectivity[40]. In Joint Communication: Connecting Europe and Asia – Building Blocks for an EU Strategy the European Commission pledged to further promote Erasmus and the Marie Skłodowska Curie actions and related reciprocity arrangements to increase opportunities for exchange and mobility in Asia.

The EU recognizes the Indo-Pacific region's growing economic, demographic, and political weight which makes it a key player in shaping the rules-based international order and in addressing global challenges. With this new strategy and the Global Gateway, the EU aims to contribute to the region's stability, security, prosperity and sustainable development, in line with the principles of democracy, rule of law, human rights and international law. The EU Strategy for Cooperation in the Indo-Pacific will allow the EU to enhance cooperation in the following priority areas: sustainable and inclusive prosperity, digital connectivity, green transition, security and defence, ocean governance, human security and digital governance and partnerships. Korea, a like-minded strategic partner, will play a crucial role in co-implement this strategy and boost bilateral cooperation with the EU.

During the mentioned 7th meeting of the EU-Korea Joint Science & Technology Cooperation Committee on 14 February 2022, Korean authorities officially submitted a letter of intent expressing Korea's intention to start discussing Korea's membership in the Horizon Europe programme as an associated country. Korea is one of the six third countries considered to become associated with Horizon Europe together with Australia, Canada, Japan, Singapore and New Zealand. Once associated it will fundamentally change the way Korean participants are involved in Horizon Europe project. Association to EU

R&D programmes offers almost equal access and rights to non-members, in exchange for a budgetary contribution. By March 2022 Albania, Georgia, Iceland, Israel, Moldova, Montenegro, North Macedonia, Norway, Serbia and Turkey have been associated to Horizon Europe, while Bosnia and Herzegovina, Kosovo, the UK and Ukraine have signed agreements to do so.[41] It remains to be seen whether Korea will be associated to all of the Horizon Europe pillars. In any case, Korean institutions and companies will benefit from the association by being able to apply for direct funding without the condition of joining a consortium led by an entity from the EU Member States.

With or without association to Horizon Europe Korea is a like-minded partner of the European Union sharing similar values and policy objectives. One of the most crucial policy objectives commonly shared between the EU and Korea is the plan to stop producing any additional greenhouse (net-zero greenhouse gas emissions) by 2050. This objective is in line with the EU's commitment to global climate action under the Paris Agreement. The vision for a climate-neutral EU was set out by the European Commission in November 2018. This vision covers nearly all EU policies and is in line with the Paris Agreement objective to keep the global temperature increase to well below 2°C and pursue efforts to keep it to 1.5°C. As part of the European Green Deal, on 4 March 2020 the Commission proposed the first European Climate Law which is currently in the final stages of negotiation between EU institutions. The European Climate Law was published in the Official Journal on 9 July 2021 and entered into force on 29 July 2021. The law turned political commitment into a legal obligation.

Similarly, the Korean government also declared the 2050 Carbon Neutral Strategy with a net zero GHG emission target for 2050. The administration of President Moon Jae-in pledged to implement a firm national energy plan that will drastically reduce fossil fuel and nuclear energy while promoting renewable energy. The plan is also aimed at creating jobs and helping the economy recover from the coronavirus fallout as well as to include remodeling public buildings, creating urban forests, recycling, establishing a foundation for new and renewable energy, and creating low-carbon energy industrial complexes to reduce reliance on fossil fuels[42].

Conclusions

Korea's participation in the EU's Framework Programmes to boost research and innovation is still rather symbolic but has been increased step-by-step with every edition of EU's Framework Programme. This will change significantly if or when Korea becomes an associated country to Horizon Europe. The association will allow Korean entities to directly benefit from European funding schemes without the necessity to join consortia led by European partners. The Korean government will contribute to European funds according to Korea's rate of participation.

Both the EU and Korea agreed to prioritize cooperation in five thematic areas, namely ICT, Health/BIO, Climate Change and Emerging Future Technology, Research Hub, and Human capital development.

In the area of ICT, two Joint Call projects have been conducted in 2016 and 2018 respectively. Korea also introduced the Digital New Deal Initiative, upgraded to integrate Korea's ICT policy, proposed Beyond-5G/6G, Cloud-Edge/ AI, Cyber Security, Quantum as potential fields of the third EU-Korea ICT Joint Calls in 2023. The EU also suggested that the EU-Korea consultation could take place under the Digital Partnership framework.

In future areas of cooperation in Health/Bio, in February 2022, Korea proposed developing and sharing animal models for COVID-19 infection, and jointly analyzing and sharing preclinical data from COVID-19 infection. The EU side emphasizes the importance of international cooperation in antibiotic resistance research, briefed on the European One Health Antimicrobial (OH AMR) Partnership, and expressed hope for Korea to participate in the OH AMR as a partner country.

As far as climate change and emerging future technologies are concerned, the EU undersigns the synergies between Korea' Carbon Neutrality and Green Growth Act for the Climate Change (CNGGA) and EU initiatives on driving decarbonization of cities: Horizon Europe Climate Neutral and Smart Cities Mission and Urban Transitions Mission developed with Mission Innovation. Synergies are also possible between Korea's CNGGA and two missions of Mission Innovation: Net-zero industries and Integrated Biorefineries using the recent announcements like the "Carbon Neutrality Vision and Strategy for Industry and Energy": achieve carbon neutrality in the industry and energy sectors.

Opportunities for cooperation with Korea on human capital development have also been increasing and are expected to increase, in particular through the MSCA for the training, mobility and career development of researchers, and the setting up of excellent doctoral programs. The EU sees a lot of room for improvement in cooperation, with positive benefits on both European and Korean organizations and researchers. During the JSTCC meeting the EU expressed willingness to hold working-level videoconference meetings to follow up after the JSTCC to exchange information and strengthen cooperation, a suggestion which was welcomed by the Korean Ministry o Science and ICT.

The EU and Korea could join their forces and forge the agenda of peaceful R&I cooperation under multilateral arrangement at the G20, ASEM, and UN Framework Convention on Climate Change. Both parties can be considered a middle power and must find their way to develop and seek for solution the solution to the most pending global issues in the international system driven by G2 rivalry and destabilized by the recent Russian invasion of Ukraine.

---

1 The Republic of Korea or South Korea.

2 "Research Projects under Framework Programmes," accessed February 7, 2021, https://ec.europa.eu/eurostat/cros/content/research-projects-under-framework-programmes-0_en.

3 "European Research Council," accessed February 6, 2021, https://erc.europa.eu/.

4 "Science Business, HORIZON BLOG," accessed February 7, 2021, https://marie-sklodowska-curie-actions.ec.europa.eu/news/msca-announces-eu822-million-for-researchers-and-organisations-in-2021.; "European Commission, MSCA," accessed February 6, 2021, https://ec.europa.eu/research/mariecurieactions/msca-actions_en.

5 "European Strategy Forum on Research Infrastructures," accessed February 6, 2021, http://roadmap2018.esfri.eu/.

6 "Excellence Science Budget," accessed February 6, 2021, https://www.catalyze-group.com/fund/horizon-europe/budget/.

7 "Global challenges and European industrial competitiveness,", accessed February 6, 2021, https://www.vinnova.se/en/m/horisont-europa/industrial-competitiveness/.; "Horizon Europe – Global Challenges & European Industrial Competitiveness pillar," accessed February 6, 2021, https://www.catalyze-group.com/fund/horizon-europe/global-challenges-european-industrial-competitiveness/.

8 "The European Innovation Council," accessed February 6, 2021, https://ec.europa.eu/info/sites/info/files/research_and_innovation/knowledge_publications_tools_and_data/documents/ec_rtd_factsheet-eic_2019.pdf.

9 "European Regions Research and Innovation," accessed February 6, 2021, https://errin.eu/RI-Policy/european-innovation-ecosystems-horizon-europe-pillar-iii.

10 "The European Institute of Innovation & Technology," accessed February 6, 2021, https://eit.europa.eu/.

11 "Researchers and a Code of Conduct," accessed February 6, 2021, https://euraxess.ec.europa.eu/euraxess/charter-code-researchers.

12 "EURAXESS," accessed February 6, 2021, https://euraxess.ec.europa.eu/.

13 "EU support for open access," accessed February 7, 2021, https://ec.europa.eu/info/research-and-innovation/strategy/goals-research-and-innovation-policy/open-science/open-access_en.

14 "Horizon Europe Strategic Plan (2021-2024)," accessed April 24, 2022, https://ec.europa.eu/info/research-and-innovation/strategy/goals-research-and-innovation-policy/open-science/open-access_en.

15 "Horizon Europe," accessed February 7, 2021, https://ec.europa.eu/information_society/newsroom/image/document/2019-29/2__eu-china_expert_seminar_25_0_2019_-_horizon_europe_9C520929-E724-5F7E-A1C84067CAE768DE_60878.pdf.

16 "Mission area: Adaptation to climate change including societal transformation," accessed February 7, 2021, https://ec.europa.eu/info/horizon-europe/missions-horizon-europe/adaptation-climate-change-including-societal-transformation_en.

17 "Conquering Cancer: Mission possible," accessed February 7, 2021, https://op.europa.eu/en/web/eu-law-and-publications/publication-detail/-/publication/d0235612-b68a-11ea-bb7a-01aa75ed71a1.

18 "Cancer: a critical challenge," accessed February 7, 2021, https://ec.europa.eu/info/horizon-europe/missions-horizon-europe/cancer_en,

19 "Heslinki Manifesto," accessed April 24, 2022, https://www.scribd.com/document/290101063/Helsinki-Manifesto-201106.

20 "Living Labs," accessed April 24, 2022, https://s3platform-legacy.jrc.ec.europa.eu/living-labs.

21 "EU Mission: A Soil Deal for Europe," accessed April 24, 2022, https://ec.europa.eu/info/research-and-innovation/funding/funding-opportunities/funding-programmes-and-open-calls/horizon-europe/eu-missions-horizon-europe/soil-health-and-food_en.

22 "Caring for soil is caring for life, " accessed February 7, 2022, https://op.europa.eu/en/publication-detail/-/publication/32d5d312-b689-11ea-bb7a-01aa75ed71a1/language-en/format-PDF/source-150223991.

23 "100 climate-neutral cities by 2030 - by and for the citizens, " accessed February 7, 2021, https://

op.europa.eu/en/publication-detail/-/publication/82f1df57-b68b-11ea-bb7a-01aa75ed71a1/language-en/format-PDF/source-150223552.

24 "European Commission, Directorate-General for Research and Innovation, *Regenerating our ocean and waters by 2030 : interim report of the mission board healthy oceans, seas, coastal and inland waters*, Publications Office, 2020," accessed April 24, 2022, https://op.europa.eu/en/publication-detail/-/publication/d0246783-b68a-11ea-bb7a-01aa75ed71a1/language-en/format-PDF/source-150222923.

25 "All data derived from Horizon 2020 Dashboard," accessed April 24, 2022, https://webgate.ec.europa.eu/dashboard/sense/app/a976d168-2023-41d8-acec-e77640154726/sheet/d23bba31-e385-4cc0-975e-a67059972142/state/analysis.

26 Proposals that have not failed at the eligibility admissibility step of the evaluation, that have not been withdrawn, that are not duplicates nor not fully evaluated yet.

27 Agreements signed, including suspended, terminated, and closed grant agreements.

28 Funding received by the project's participants after deduction of their linked third parties' funding.

29 The act of involvement of a legal entity in a grant agreement. A single participant can be involved in N grant agreements and therefore being counted as N participants.

30 One organization participating in N projects is only counted once.

31 - All high-quality proposals submitted to the Horizon 2020 SME Instrument, which are above the quality threshold, but cannot be funded under the available budget;

- MSCA-IF proposals, starting with the 2016 call, that obtained a score of 85% or more;

- Special COVID-19 Response Seal of Excellence awarded to COVID-19 relevant proposals submitted to the March 2020 EIC Accelerator cut-off which passed the thresholds but were not funded.

By default, the dashboards show only the proposals which at the moment of the data extraction appear still unfunded; additionally, the data is filtered at the level of the coordinator.

32 A collaborative link is assumed to exist between each pair of participants in each contract. The number of collaborative links created by a project is calculated in the following way:(a) When there are n participants from a given country in a project, the number of collaborative links between participants from the given country formed as a result of the project is assumed to be n*(n-1)/2.(b) When there are m participants from one country and p from another country in a project, the number of collaborative links created between the two countries as a result of the project is assumed to be m*p.

33 "CORDIS," accessed April 25, 2022, https://cordis.europa.eu/project/id/731884.

34 "CORDIS," accessed April 25, 2022, https://cordis.europa.eu/project/id/825496.

35 "CORDIS," accessed April 25, 2022, https://cordis.europa.eu/project/id/731993.

36 "CORDIS," accessed April 25, 2022, https://cordis.europa.eu/project/id/643381.

37 "CORDIS," accessed April 25, 2022, https://cordis.europa.eu/project/id/727890.

38 Number of SMEs applying for H2020 grants through calls of proposals. One SME applying in N proposals in counted N times.

39 "EUREKA Network," accessed March 6, 2022, https://www.eurekanetwork.org/.

40 "Joint Communication: Connecting Europe and Asia – Building Blocks for an EU Strategy," accessed April 24, 2022, https://www.eeas.europa.eu/sites/default/files/joint_communication_-_connecting_europe_and_asia_-_building_blocks_for_an_eu_strategy_2018-09-19.pdf.

41 "South Korea to begin talks on Horizon Europe association," accessed March 6, 2022, https://www.researchprofessionalnews.com/rr-news-europe-horizon-2020-2022-2-south-korea-to-begin-talks-on-horizon-europe-association/.

42 "South Korea's Moon targets carbon neutrality by 2050," accessed March 6, 2022, https://www.reuters.com/article/us-southkora-environment-greenewdeal-idUSKBN27D1DU.

List of Contributors

Axel Berkofsky is Professor at the University of Pavia and Co-Head of Asia Center at ISPI, Milan. Berkofsky is also a regular contributor to the Zurich-based International Security Network (ISN), the Asia Times, as well as to other newspapers, journals and magazines on Asian politics and security, EU-Asia relations, Japanese domestic and foreign, Chinese foreign policies and North Korea.

Nicola Casarini is associate fellow at the Istituto Affari Internazionali (IAI) and Global Fellow at the Wilson Center in Washington DC. He obtained PhD in International Relation at LSE. He has held positions at the Graduate Institute in Geneva, at the EU Institute for Security Studies in Paris, at Bocconi University in Milan, at the European University Institute in Florence. Nicola is the founder and director of Orientedworld.com, a global consultancy platform.

Kang Yoo-Duk is a Professor in economics of the Division of Language and Trade at Hankuk University of Foreign Studies (HUFS) and is a editor of the Asia Pacific Journal of EU studies. Prof. Kang received his doctorate from Science Po Paris. He worked as a research fellow and team leader of the Europe department at the Korea Institute for International Economic Policy (KIEP), Korea. His main research interest is trade policy, economic integration, and comparative studies of economic policies.

Kim Bongchul is Professor of Division of International Studies at the Hankuk University of Foreign Studies (HUFS) and Director of EU Research Institute at HUFS. Kim received doctorate from King's College London and is also a regular contributor to the Korea Legal Research Institute (KLRI) as well as to other newspapers, journals and magazines on Asian and Korean laws and international relations.

Kim Sihong is Jean Monnet Professor of EU Studies Department of the GSIAS at the Hankuk University of Foreign Studies (HUFS), Seoul, Korea. He obtained MA and PhD from Gregorian University, Rome. Currently he is Dean of the College of European Studies and also Director of the HUFS Jean Monnet Centre of Excellence supported by the European Union. He was president of the Korean Society of Contemporary European Studies (KSCES) in 2009. In 2013, Prof. Kim was decorated as a Cavaliere, Order of Merit of the Italian Republic.

Lee Moosung is Professor of the Department of Political Science and Diplomacy, Myongji university, Seoul, Korea. He has his PhD at the University of Birmingham, UK, and since then has undertaken a variety of academic and public services. Mostly recently, he has served as president of the Korean Society of Contemporary European Studies. His research interests are wide-ranging, from small states and EU enlargement to the EU-Korea relations, and his research outputs have also been widely published both as journal articles and monographs.

Tereza Novotna is a Korea-Europe Center Fellow at Free University of Berlin. She is also a Senior Associate Research Fellow at the EUROPEUM, a Prague-based think-tank. In 2017-2018, Tereza was a Korea Foundation Visiting Professor at Seoul National University. She received her doctorate from Boston University in 2012. She has widely published on EU foreign policy in Journal of Common Market Studies, Studia Diplomatica, and on the EU-Northeast Asia relations in 38th North, The Diplomat, The Bulletin of the Atomic Scientists, 9DashLine and others.

Michael Reiterer is Distinguished Professor, Centre for Security, Diplomacy & Strategy, Brussels School of Governance. He was Former Ambassador of the European Union to the Republic of Korea, having previously held the position of Principal Advisor at the Asia and Pacific Department, European External Action Service (EEAS), Brussels, in charge of strategic and security matters. He previously served as EU Ambassador to Switzerland and the Principality of Liechtenstein (2007-2011), Minister/Deputy Head of the EU-Delegation to Japan (2002-2006), and ASEM Counselor (1998-2002).

Ramon Pacheco Pardo is KF-VUB Korea Chair at the Centre for Security, Diplomacy and Strategy (CSDS) of the VUB Brussels School of Governance. He is also Professor of International Relations at King's College London. He is an Adjunct Fellow (Non-Resident) with the Korea Chair at CSIS, Non-Resident Fellow with Sejong Institute, and Committee Member at CSCAP EU. Prof. Pacheco Pardo has held visiting positions at Korea University, the Lee Kuan Yew School of Public Policy, and Melbourne University.

Tomasz Wierzbowski holds a Ph.D. in International Relations from Hankuk University of Foreign Studies and MA in International Politics obtained at Sungkyunkwan University under Korean Government Scholarship. He is focused on the Northeast Asia region and offers academic courses in International Relations and Comparative Politics. His academic interest lies also in the methodology of the social sciences. Tomasz is currently Head of EURAXESS Korea.

Connecting Europe and Asia

Security, Economy and Mobility

Author	Sihong Kim and Michael Reiterer
First Printed	2023.03.15
First Published	2023.03.21
Director	Yunsung Koh
Executive Contents Creator	Sunho Shin
Contents Creator	Haejung Jang Jaeeun Roh Daeun Byun
Designer	Sunah Choi Daewook Kim
Published by	HANKUK UNIVERSITY OF FOREIGN STUDIES KNOWLEDGE CONTENTS & PRESS 107, Imun-ro, Dongdaemun-gu, Seoul 02450, Korea Tel.) 82-2-2173-2497 Fax.) 82-2-2173-3363 E-mail) press@hufs.ac.kr Online) http://press.hufs.ac.kr
Printed by	Twinbell Tel.) 82-2-2088-1810
ISBN	979-11-5901-713-1 [93340]
Price	20,000 Won